DEFEATING THE NEW AXIS POWERS

Same Plot New Script New Cast Same Ending

JAMES MICHAEL MATTHEW

Archway Publishing books may be ordered through booksellers or by contacting:

Archway Publishing
1663 Liberty Drive
Bloomington, IN 47403
www.archwaypublishing.com
844-669-3957

ISBN: 978-1-6657-3688-6 (sc)
ISBN: 978-1-6657-3687-9 (hc)
ISBN: 978-1-6657-3689-3 (e)

Library of Congress Control Number: 2023901734

Print information available on the last page.

Archway Publishing rev. date: 1/31/2023

This book is dedicated to all the people of the
world living under totalitarian regimes.

CONTENTS

ACKNOWLEDGMENTS

I want to acknowledge all the people in Ukraine for fighting the fight for all of us. I look forward to visiting your country someday and establishing an office there as you rebuild your great and free society.

INTRODUCTION

Defeating the New Axis Powers is the second of a three-part series dedicated to providing new solutions for solving the critical problems brought by global warming, climate change, rising ocean coastlines, biodiversity loss, desertification, ocean pollution, and freshwater depletion. This book focuses on the geopolitical issues related to climate change. My fifth book and the third of this series, *The Two $20 Trillion Opportunities*, focuses on paying for climate change and preparing for *The Selfless Economy*. My third book, *Building the Climate Change Bridge*, built the bridge for how we can transition from fossil fuels to green-energy-based societies—a bridge for how we get there from here.

As you begin this book, you might think to yourself, *Why am I reading a book about politics and World War III? I want to study climate change and global warming.* Or you might think, *I want to read about politics. Why am I reading about climate change?* The answer to both questions is that country-by-country politics and geopolitics collectively are all connected to climate change. Energy policy must consider both climate change and geopolitics. Not all countries of the world "play by the rules." The new Axis powers are more than happy to play with the West under the pretense of caring about achieving net-zero carbon, but all along, they have been weaponizing fossil fuels and green energy's raw materials under the disguise of embracing green energy. So long as we understand the geopolitical chessboard, we can defeat the new Axis powers and global warming simultaneously. But defeating the new Axis powers must always take precedent over defeating global warming.

1

World War III Has Already Begun

IT IS NO secret that the new Axis powers hate the US. They hate us for our status as a global super power since winning World War II and the Cold War. They hate us for our commitment to individual freedom. The new Axis powers believe their totalitarian forms of government will prevail in the twenty-first century and beyond. China is the ring leader and most often picked to surpass the United States' status as the number one economic power. For those of you who do not understand that World War III has already started or who naively believe climate change should take priority over defeating the new Axis powers, you do not need to take my word for it. Just read the following:

- "Putin's State TV Propagandist Olga Skabeyeva Says 'World War III Has Already Begun'"[1]
- "'World War III Has Begun after Sinking of Moskva': Russian State TV"[2]
- "Bill Ackman Says Russia's Attack on Ukraine Means World War III Has Likely Already Started"[3]

- "DNA Special: Has World War III Already Begun?"[4]
- "Are We Heading for World War Three?"[5]
- "Pope Francis: 'World War III Has Been Declared'"[6]
- "China Threatens 'Strong Measures' if Pelosi Visits Taiwan"[7]
- "China Warns Taiwan Independence Would Trigger War"[8]
- "America's Top Brass Responds to the Threat of China in the Pacific"[9]
- "Iran's Military Warns U.S. against Threats to Use Force"[10]
- "Exclusive: U.S. Government Warns That Iran May Try to Kill American Officials as Revenge for Killing Top General"[11]
- "Nicaragua Authorizes Entry of Russian Troops, Planes, Ships"[12]
- "Putin Forges Ties with Iran's Supreme Leader in Tehran Talks"[13]
- "The China Threat"

> The counterintelligence and economic espionage efforts emanating from the government of China and the Chinese Communist Party are a grave threat to the economic well-being and democratic values of the United States. Confronting this threat is the FBI's top counterintelligence priority. To be clear, the adversary is not the Chinese people or people of Chinese descent or heritage. The threat comes from the programs and policies pursued by an authoritarian government. The Chinese government is employing tactics that seek to influence lawmakers and public opinion to achieve policies that are more favorable to China. At the same time, the Chinese government is seeking to become the world's greatest superpower through predatory lending and business practices,

systematic theft of intellectual property, and brazen cyber intrusions. China's efforts target businesses, academic institutions, researchers, lawmakers, and the general public and will require a whole-of-society response. The government and the private sector must commit to working together to better understand and counter the threat.

"Made in Beijing: The Plan for Global Market Domination"

Through interviews with FBI agents and executives of victim companies, this film aims to help the private sector recognize the urgent need to protect their intellectual property against sustained and ongoing industrial espionage by the People's Republic of China (PRC). Visit fbi.gov/china threat to learn more.

"The greatest long-term threat to our nation's information and intellectual property, and to our economic vitality, is the counterintelligence and economic espionage threat from China." (FBI Director Christopher Wray) [14]

- "China Warns US after Tracking Warship in South China Sea"[15]
- "China Threatens Nuclear War, Expanding Arsenal in Case of 'Intense Showdown' with US"[16]
- "China Warns US Not to Include Taiwan in Indo-Pacific Strategy"[17]
- "China's Growing Firepower Casts Doubt on Whether U.S. Could Defend Taiwan"[18]

- "'Day Will Come Soon': China Threatens US of Hawaii Incursion for Entering South China Sea"[19]
- "China Warns US It Will Be Defeated if the Two Superpowers Go to War"[20]
- "China Threatens to 'Hunt Down' US Military Jets if They Again Land in Taiwan"[21]
- "The US-China Cold War Has Already Started"[22]
- "China Warns U.S. against Forming Pacific NATO and Backing Taiwan"[23]

I could have added much more. I could have gone on and on, but I have seen enough. If the previous material is not enough for you, add your own research. You will not run out of material to read.

2

Defining the Opposing Side

Axis Powers of the Past

EVERY FEW DECADES, dictators and self-serving power narcissists from Europe, Asia, and the Middle East get together with the collective belief that they can conquer the free world and end democracy on the planet. The Axis powers in World War II were Germany, Italy, and Japan. Axis powers in World War I included Germany, Austria-Hungary, Bulgaria, and the Ottoman Empire. In the Crimean War, Russia fought against Britain, France, and the Ottoman Empire. In the end, democratic societies always won out, and the dictators lost.

The New Axis Powers

Unfortunately, here we go again. History is repeating itself with the new Axis powers, who believe they have got it right this time. They believe that a new world order has been formed, where a few totalitarians at the top rule over everyone else, and their armies are beholden to them, rather than the people of those nations. A new world order that weaponizes energy and other natural resources. This new world order would have no pendulums of society to correct their errors and bad ideas. Instead it would perpetuate bad linear thinking until it finally destroyed itself.

For more information, read the following articles: "Putin Accused the US of Acting like God and Predicted a New World Order in Bullish St Petersburg Speech" and "Chinese President Xi Jinping Has Vowed to Lead the 'New World Order.'"[24]

So what countries make up what I am calling the new Axis powers, and what are the criteria to be included? The criteria for inclusion are the desire to end the United States and its democratic allies and to possess nuclear weapons. Therefore, the new Axis powers include China, Russia, Iran, and North Korea. For more evidence, please read the following articles:

- "China Touts Relationship with Russia, Accuses US of Being 'Main Instigator of the Ukrainian Crisis'"[25]
- "Putin Tells Kim Jong-Un That They Will Expand 'Constructive Bilateral Relations,' North Korea Says"[26]
- "Iran's Top Automaker Sets Sights on Russian Market Following Sanctions"[27]
- "Ukraine War Round-Up: Strike on Wagner HQ and Russia to Increase Ties with North Korea"[28]
- "Russian Embassy Praises Chinese Drone as 'Symbol of Modern Warfare'"[29]
- "Game of Drones: Iran Hosts UAV Competition with Russia and Belarus"[30]
- "Putin Knows He Made 'Mistake' with Ukraine, Will Never Admit It: Stavridis"[31]
- "China, Russia to Engage in Joint Military Exercise"[32]
- "Iran-Linked Hacking Group Is Targeting Israeli Shipping, US Cybersecurity Firm Says"[33]
- "Russia Grows Closer to North Korea amid International Isolation"[34]
- "Russian Navy Should Be Equipped with Tactical Nukes, Says Russian Scientist"[35]

- "Iran Is Already Nuclearized, so Why Do We Need a Deal?"[36]

Friends of the New Axis Powers

The new Axis powers have a group of countries, organizations, and individuals that support them and are not democracies, but they do not have nuclear weapons. I call this group the friends of the new Axis powers. It includes Mexican drug cartels, human traffickers, crime organizations around the world, drug traffickers, and money launderers. Syria, Belarus, Cuba, Venezuela, and Nicaragua are also included. For more information, see the following articles:

- "Putin Scrambling for Support from 'Outcasts' Shows His Weakness: Expert"[37]
- "Idaho Sheriff Sends Dire Warning to 'Idiotic' Biden Officials: 'We Are on the Cusp of Complete Collapse'"[38]
- "Hundreds of Mexican National Guard Troops Sent to Tijuana over Cartel-Fueled Violence"[39]
- "2 Years after Dictator Lukashenko Stole the Election, Belarus Is a Grim Place"[40]
- "Putin Offers 'Most Advanced' Weapons to Socialist Triad in Latin America"[41]
- "Venezuela Halts Oil Shipments to Europe, Demands New Concessions"[42]

Unofficially Neutral Powers

There is a third group that contains countries that do not officially support the new Axis powers but do not hesitate to partner with them when it is convenient to do so. Countries that generally fall into this category include the following:

- Brazil;
- India;
- South Africa;
- Argentina;

- Indonesia; and
- Others from time to time, depending on the situation.

For more information, read the following:

- "Emerging Markets Rush to Join BRICS Alliance as High Energy Prices Persist"[43]
- "Russia Displaces Saudi Arabian Oil in India"[44]
- "Xi Jinping's Saudi Trip Seeks to Exploit Riyadh-Washington Tensions"[45]
- "Chinese President Due in Saudi Arabia to Tighten Economic Ties"[46]
- "China, India Hold 16th Corps Commander Level Meeting on Border Issues"[47]
- "China, Uzbekistan to Hold 6th Meeting of Intergovernmental Cooperation Committee"[48]
- "Chinese, Canadian FMs Vow to Bring Bilateral Relations 'Back on Track'"[49]
- "China, Chile Vow to Push Bilateral Relations to Higher Level"[50]
- "China Is World's 2nd Largest Commercial Satellite Owner"[51]
- "How China's Propaganda Influences the West"[52]

Allies

As in the past, the Allies are comprised of the major democracies of the world. The current major countries include the members of NATO and European Union Countries, Japan, Australia, South Korea, and Israel. For more information, read the following articles:

- "UK Summons Chinese Ambassador over 'Aggressive' Escalation on Taiwan"[53]
- "U.S. Joins South Korea, Australia, Japan, Canada for Missile Defense Exercise Following RIMPAC"[54]
- "US to Hold Wide-Ranging Trade Talks with Taiwan amid Tensions with China"[55]

- "Next North Korea Nuclear Test Could Lead US to Deploy 'Strategic Assets' to South Korea, Two Allies Say"[56]

Blood Enemies of the New Axis Powers

The new Axis powers have a long list of blood enemies from their histories of murder, war, rape, imprisonment, and other acts of genocide against oppressed populations under their heels of totalitarianism. These blood enemies include Belarus insurgents, Chechnya insurgents, Kurds, Georgia dissidents, 3.8 million slave workers in China, Chinese dissidents in PRC and abroad, Hong Kong dissidents, Russian dissidents, and families of Russian soldiers who fought in the Ukraine War. These people are just waiting in the wings for their opportunity to settle old scores. For more information, see the following:

- "Russian Families Descend on the Kremlin to Demand Truth about Soldiers"[57]
- "Hackers Linked to China Have Been Targeting Human Rights Groups for Years"

  The hackers, known as RedAlpha, have taken aim at organizations including Amnesty International, the International Federation for Human Rights, Radio Free Asia, the Mercator Institute for China Studies, and other think tanks and government and humanitarian groups around the world. [58]
- "Hong Kong Two Years after the Passage of the National Security Act"

  From all appearances, China has succeeded in bringing its wayward Special Autonomous Region to heel. Democracy activists are either in prison or living in asylum abroad, subject to harassment by pro-Chinese forces. For the United States and its allies in Asia, there are sobering lessons to be learned from China's recent approach to Hong Kong.[59]
- "Iranian Dissidents Rally This Weekend in Albania as Washington-Tehran Tensions Surge"

The world's biggest exiled Iranian dissident movement will hold its annual rally this weekend to call for regime change in Iran and to push the U.S. and Western nations to adopt a firmer policy rather than seek negotiations and diplomacy with Tehran."[60]

Reluctant Friends and Closet Enemies of the New Axis Powers

There are also many countries around the world that would rather see the new Axis powers taken down but are reluctant or afraid to do so. These countries include most Eurasian, Middle Eastern, and Pacific Rim countries not listed elsewhere. Information on this can be found in the article "China's Xi Considers Visiting Central Asia, Potential Meeting with Putin Next Month" from the *Wall Street Journal*.[61]

Weaponizing Energy with Fossil Fuels at the Tip of the Spear

Why must we study and consider the new Axis powers when studying climate change and energy policy? The new Axis powers understand the importance of access to energy for a country and society to function. They hate the US and all democracies around the world. They believe their totalitarian forms of government will prevail in their self-envisioned new world order.

Global conflicts over energy are not new. Japan's attack on Pearl Harbor was about energy. But what differs this time around is the new Axis powers all have nuclear weapons. Unfortunately, the world is at a real risk of nuclear weapons being detonated. Global warming must take a back seat to defeating the new Axis powers. The geopolitics of energy policy cannot be denied. They must be included in any strategy that has a remote hope of ultimate success. For more information, read "How Russian Oil Is Making Its Way from Europe to Asia" from *Oil Price*.[62]

Russia's Invasion of Ukraine Has Changed Everything

Russia's invasion of Ukraine has opened the eyes of the world and laid bare the folly of net-zero carbon's attempt at globalization and top-down policy making. The invasion of Ukraine has also uncovered the true intentions of the new Axis powers—to control the world by destroying America and its allies. Information on this can be found in the following articles:

- "Russian Defense Minister: 'Soon Soviet Union Will Return'"[63]
- "Putin Regime at 'Beginning of the End': Russia Expert"[64]
- "Tshibaka to Newsmax: Alaskans 'Very Concerned' Over NORAD Report"

> Alaskans are "very concerned" by the news this week that North American Aerospace Defense Command (NORAD) detected Russian surveillance aircraft flying twice into the Alaskan Air Defense Identification Zone, Kelly Tshibaka, one of the candidates for the U.S. Senate in the state, commented on Newsmax Friday.[65]

Putin's Rubicon Circle Moment

In chapter 1 of my second book, *Reject Self-Serving Power*, I discussed how self-serving power strategies always fail in the end. In the second chapter of that book, I discussed what I have termed the Rubicon circles of power and time. The invasion of Ukraine will go down in history as Putin's Rubicon circle moment. Excerpts from my second book are as follows:

Crossing the Rubicon Circle

> Most people are familiar with the phrase "crossing the Rubicon." For those who are not, it began with Julius Caesar's crossing the Rubicon River in Italy in 49 BC to cross into Rome. This led to Caesar becoming dictator of Rome. I have borrowed this phrase to explain what I call the Rubicon circles of power and time. These circles represent periods of time that all self-serving power individuals eventually encounter.

Inner Circle: Period of Positive Results

As previously discussed, many power strategies yield positive results in their early stages. These positive results almost always occur as the result of replacing an already existing crisis, corrupt regime, or unpopular or negative period in history. Hamilton and Burr had the election of 1800. Adolf Hitler had the Great Depression and the Treaty of Versailles. Joseph Stalin had Hitler. Al Capone and Bugsy Malone had Prohibition.

Corruption Circle: Period of Decline Due to Power Corruption

This is the time period during which the accumulation of self-serving power corrupts the self-serving-power-driven individual.

Rubicon Circle

The date when the self-serving power individual commits a code-red moment (see Book 1) is that person's Rubicon—the date that person's fate is sealed. This individual will fail and be removed—generally in disgrace or even dead. Unfortunately, as with Caesar crossing the Rubicon River, the pain does not end on the date of the Rubicon circle crossing. There will be a subsequent period of clinging to power at all cost, during which everyone is negatively impacted. A diagram of the Rubicon circles is included in Figure 1.

Figure 1

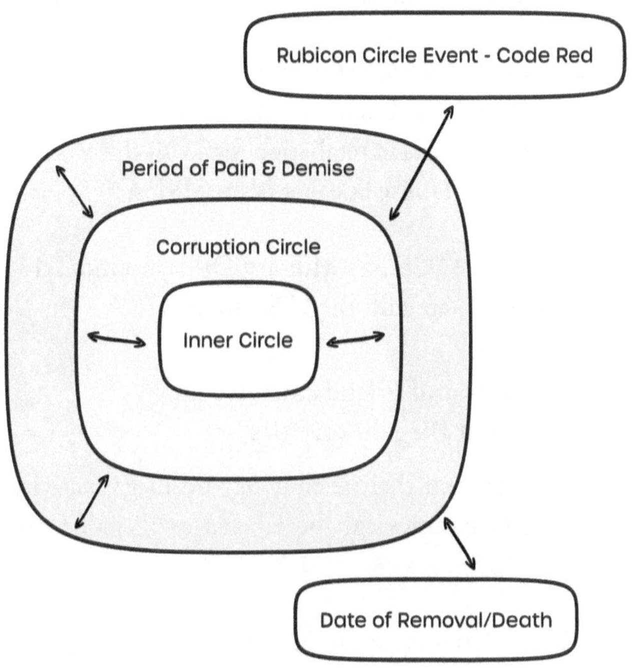

Rubicon Circles of Power and Time
Rubicon Circle Event - Code Red
Period of Pain & Demise
Corruption Circle
Inner Circle
Date of Removal/Death

Taiwan Will Be China's Ukraine and Xi's Rubicon Circle Moment

Russia's invasion of Ukraine will prove to be, to the new Axis powers in World War III, what Pearl Harbor was to Germany and the Axis powers during World War II. Much like Adolf Hitler's declaration of war on the US after Japan attacked Pearl Harbor, China's Xi has essentially declared war on America through Taiwan. Taiwan will be Xi's Rubicon circle. History's self-serving power dictators, tyrants, and political criminals cannot help themselves. They have been corrupted over time and travel down a linear pathway, unchecked by the three pendulums protecting democratic societies. For more information, read the following excerpt from the article "China Halts Climate, Military Ties over Pelosi Taiwan Visit":

> China says it is canceling or suspending dialogue with the U.S. on issues from climate change to military relations and anti-drug efforts in retaliation for a visit this week to Taiwan by U.S. House Speaker Nancy Pelosi.[66]

Also read the article "China's Military Drills around Taiwan Show How It Is Closing the Gap with the U.S." from *NPR*.[67]

The New Axis Powers and Friends Survive on Illegal Economies and Illegal Activities

The new Axis powers and their friends rely on illegal activities to the point where their economies can be labeled as illegal. Consider the following:

- "The China Connection in Mexico's Illegal Economies" Increasingly, Chinese actors and markets are thickly intertwined in Mexico's illegal economies, such as drug and wildlife trafficking and money laundering.[68]
- "Forced Labor in China's Xinjiang Region" Over the last four years, the People's Republic of China (PRC) has carried out a mass detention and political indoctrination campaign against Uyghurs, who are

predominantly Muslim, and members of other ethnic and religious minority groups in the Xinjiang Uyghur Autonomous Region (Xinjiang), a large region in western China. The courageous voices of survivors, their family members abroad, researchers, and international advocacy groups have thoroughly documented the PRC's discriminatory use of surveillance technologies and trumped-up administrative and criminal charges to abduct and detain more than one million Muslims, including Uyghurs, ethnic Hui, ethnic Kazakhs, ethnic Kyrgyz, ethnic Tajiks, and ethnic Uzbeks, in as many as 1,200 state-run internment camps throughout Xinjiang. Detention in these camps is intended to erase ethnic and religious identities under the pretext of "vocational training." Forced labor is a central tactic used for this repression. In Xinjiang, the government is the trafficker. Authorities use threats of physical violence, forcible drug intake, physical and sexual abuse, and torture to force detainees to work in adjacent or off-site factories or worksites producing garments, footwear, carpets, yarn, food products, holiday decorations, building materials, extractives, materials for solar power equipment and other renewable energy components, consumer electronics, bedding, hair products, cleaning supplies, personal protective equipment, face masks, chemicals, pharmaceuticals, and other goods—and these goods are finding their way into businesses and homes around the world.[69]

- "UN Report: China's Mistreatment of Uyghurs Akin to Modern Slavery"[70]
- "Illegal Fishing and Physical Violence: Life aboard China's 'Devil Vessels' Revealed in New Report"

    China is carrying out illegal fishing activities across the entire globe, according to a new investigative report by the Environmental Justice Foundation.[71]

- "Chinese Hackers Took Trillions in Intellectual Property from about 30 Multinational Companies"

    A yearslong malicious cyber operation spearheaded by the notorious Chinese state actor, APT 41, has siphoned off an estimated trillions in intellectual property theft from approximately 30 multinational companies within the manufacturing, energy, and pharmaceutical sectors.[72]

- "China Is No. 1 Domestic National Security Threat and Biden Administration Won't Admit It"[73]
- "Palestinian Islamic Jihad's Rocket Barrages on Israel Trace back to 'Iran's Regional Tentacles,' Experts Say"[74]
- "Iran Has Begun Training Russia to Use Its Advanced Drones, U.S. Says"

    Training indicates Moscow plans to use Tehran's military weapons to try and seize a new aerial advantage in Ukraine.[75]

- "'China Threat' Emerges in Elections from UK to Australia"[76]
- "When Will American Businesses Wake Up to the Threat of Chinese Espionage?"[77]
- "America Wakes Up to the China Threat"[78]
- "GOP Congressman: Americans, Lawmakers Are 'Waking Up' to China Threat"[79]
- "Awaken to the China Threat: President Biden and America Must Understand the Dangers Posed by Our Asian Competitor"[80]

3

Conventional Warfare No Longer Works

HUMANS ARE THE only animals that engage in warfare. Throughout human history, different tribes and nations battled one another all over the world. History is filled with battlefields from the pharaohs of Egypt to the Roman Empire to the Vikings, Normans, and blue-painted Scots. Modern armies have marched over the same battlefields and shallow graveyards that indigenous tribes fought over for natural resources centuries ago.

For brief periods of time, large global wars supplanted constant regional battles. Unfortunately the world has now returned to its tribal past. Wars, large and small, are still waged regionally, but now they are also emerging on a global basis. And even worse, no end to this new global tribalism is anywhere near. Unlike Roman cohorts and centurions, who battled mano a mano, at least nine countries now possess approximately ten thousand nuclear missiles. The new Axis powers have nuclear weapons, regional domination objectives, and global ambitions. Their global ambitions are largely driven by the same age-old follies of self-serving power and a common objective to defeat the

United States of America. For more information, see my second book, *Reject Self-Serving Power*. Also read the article "Did War Help Societies Become Bigger and More Complex?" from *Big Think*.[81]

Russia's invasion of Ukraine has demonstrated that conventional warfare fought in the twentieth century no longer works in the twenty-first century. After watching Ukraine's outgunned and outmanned troops crush the once-vaunted Russian army, navy, and air force—thoroughly embarrassing Putin—can anyone even imagine a five-thousand-ship armada invading Normandy's offshore waters or the US Marines storming beaches on Pacific islands? They would all be slaughtered by missiles, drones, and other autonomous devices.

How does a nation without a navy defeat a "modern" navy? What does twenty-first-century warfare look like? What will be the winning strategies? To answer those questions, let us read what the *Modern War Institute at West Point* has to say:

> [Dr. Sean McFate] begins by arguing that the country has suffered from "strategic atrophy" and has failed to recognize that current circumstances are neither solely war nor solely peace.[82]

The assertion that our country suffers from strategic atrophy is not a new warning. According to the article "Mattis: U.S. Suffering 'Strategic Atrophy'" from *USNI News*:

> Speaking in Washington, D.C., retired Marine Corps Gen. James Mattis said, "the perception is we're pulling back" on America's commitment to its allies and partners, leaving them adrift in a changing world. "We have strategic atrophy."[83]

McFate and Mattis nailed it. The US is in strategic atrophy. McFate's statement that we currently live in times where peace and war coexist is especially insightful. The world's societies have returned to tribal status under the threat of nuclear weapons and detonations. War has become an everyday part of our society. As such, all major US policy decisions must be made through the lens of the ongoing coexistence of war and peace. Energy policy should especially be viewed in this manner.

Country by country, energy security must always trump any virtuous discussion of global green energy policies. As we have seen, any attempted policy simply gets countered by the new Axis powers building more coal plants, damming up international rivers, destroying fish stocks with massive illegal fishing fleets, and weaponizing energy. One could argue that the new Axis powers render net-zero carbon and ESG investing based on carbon emissions useless.

Except for precolonial indigenous tribal wars, the US has never had to endure a time when there was no such thing as war or peace. Our country has been in many wars since it was founded, but the war-and-peace psyche of American society has always been that war will be followed by a time of peace. Even the Cold War came to an end. I believe this change is the reason we suffer from strategic atrophy. Our society and people do not yet understand that we now live in a world where war and peace coexist, and that coexistence likely is destined to continue through the rest of the twenty-first century.

How does the one true super power plan for defense and defeat the new Axis powers under this change in society? Unlike tribal war societies of the past, which were generally regional in scope, we now must live in a society where war and peace coexist nonstop on a global basis. The new Axis powers create new battlefields and chaos faster than can be countered under conventional war strategies. In chapter 13, we will discuss possible strategies for the twenty-first century. For more information, read the articles "China, Russia, and the West's Crisis of Disbelief" and "A Costly Passivity toward China" from the *Wall Street Journal.*[84]

4

The Geographic Theaters of World War III

THE GEOGRAPHIC THEATERS of World War III are mostly already in place, including NATO, the EU's border with Russia, the Korean Peninsula, the Middle East, and the Asian Pacific. For more information, see the following:

- "Putin Ally Promotes Nuclear Strike on NATO to Counter Military Superiority"[85]
- "Ukraine's Southern Forces Wage a Slow Campaign to Wear the Russians Down"[86]
- "Russian Intelligence Knew That Ukrainians Would Not Welcome Russia, But Still Told the Kremlin They Would, Report Says"[87]
- "Ukrainian Attacks in Crimea Weaken Russia's Military Capacity"[88]
- "Putin Suffers Black Sea Crisis as Russia Loses $750M Flagship, Jets, Island"[89]

- "Blasts behind Russian Lines Had Major Psychological Effect on Putin—Officials"[90]
- "Ukraine war: Russia appeals for new recruits for war effort"[91]
- "U.S., South Korea Revive Live Military Drills after Four-Year Hiatus"[92]
- "U.S. Will Continue Taiwan Strait Transits, FONOPs in Western Pacific Despite Growing Tension with China"[93]
- "Taiwan Rejects China's 'One Country, Two Systems' Plan for the Island"[94]
- "Guam's Missile Defenses to Get a Massive Upgrade"[95]
- "The Army Brief: Guam Missile Defense; CENTCOM Contest; New Social-Media Rules; and More"

  > The Missile Defense Agency wants to find the perfect spot for a command-and-control facility on Guam, where Army cruise missile defense and other weapons are to help protect U.S. interests in the Pacific.[96]

- "Taiwan's 'Porcupine Strategy' to Fight a Potential Chinese Invasion Is Learning Lessons from Ukraine, Report Says"[97]
- "'New Normal' across the Taiwan Strait as China Threat Looms Ever Closer"[98]

The new Axis powers are trying to establish new World War III geographic theaters in order to force the US to respond. These new geographic theaters include South American countries like Nicaragua, Venezuela, and Argentina; Caribbean countries like Haiti and Cuba; Africa; and Islamic extremists. For more information, read the following:

- "Iran and a Suspicious Flight to Argentina"[99]
- "China Is Building a Nuclear Power Plant in Argentina as It Looks to Latin America"[100]
- "China Riding the 'Pink Tide' in South America"

  > China is South America's largest trading partner and Latin America's major foreign investor. Taking advantage of

> the rising Left in the continent, Beijing is strengthening bilateral ties in America's backyard.[101]

- "China May Seek Greater Role in Haiti as UN Security Council Extends Political Mission"[102]
- "Russian Mercenaries Project the Kremlin's Power Far from Its Troubles in Ukraine"

> Wagner Group, a private army formed by "Putin's Chef," takes aim at Mali's mineral riches in strategic part of Africa; allegedly involved in six massacres.[103]

- "Petraeus: Afghanistan Likely Will Be 'Incubator for Islamist Extremism' for Years"[104]

The new Axis powers are also trying to establish new geographic theaters across the US mainland. This is done through Chinese supplied drug cartels, human traffickers, and money launderers; the Chinese infiltration of elected officials, bureaucrats, colleges, and private citizens; and the buying of real estate near US military bases. For more information, read the articles "National Security Concerns Arise as China Buys Up U.S. Farmland" from *Komo News* and "Russia Uses FBI Trump Raid to 'Foment Discord' and 'Amplify Tensions' in US, Expert Says" from *Fox News*.[105]

In order to defeat the new Axis powers, the US must maintain a global framework of established and active military bases. The US currently has a large global infrastructure of military bases. Many people question the need for this many bases, but they are wrong. The US needs to continue to expand its global base readiness, not reduce it. For more information, read the article "U.S. Space Command Basing Decision Approaching Final Stretch" from *Space News*.[106] Also see this excerpt from "How Many US Military Bases Are There in the World?" from the *Soldier Project*:

> There are roughly 750 US foreign military bases; they are spread across 80 nations! After the U.S is the UK, but they only have 145 bases. Russia has about 3 dozen bases, and China just five. This implies that the U.S

has three times as many bases as all other countries combined.[107]

China Belt and Road Initiative

See the following: "China's Massive Belt and Road Initiative" from *Council on Foreign Relations*; "China's Investment Setbacks in Panama" from *The Diplomat*; and "Why a Chinese Ship's Arrival in Sri Lanka Has Caused Alarm in India and the West" from *NPR*.[108]

Forward Military Base Readiness in the Pacific Theaters

Ukraine's success against Russia has shown how important advance positioning is, especially small special-forces groups that train local country forces. There is a critical need to have advanced jungle-trained special forces to form a first line in the Pacific should the time come again. For more information, read the articles "Another Russian Spy Busted in Ukraine" from *Ukrinform*; "Southeast Asia Seeks to Tiptoe through U.S.-China Taiwan Minefield" from the *Wall Street Journal*; and "U.S. Navy Is Seeing More 'Unsafe' Aerial Intercepts by China, Says Seventh Fleet Commander" from *CNBC*.[109]

Climate Change Lakes and Climate Change Islands

As discussed in chapter 21 of my second book, *Reject Self-Serving Power*, climate change lakes and climate change islands can serve to expand World War III battlefields in favor of the Allies. This topic will be discussed further in chapter 13.

Regime Change Movements inside the Four Axis Powers

The most important geographic theaters of World War III will be inside the borders of the new Axis powers. Movements for regime changes that are driven largely by internal opposing forces and ideologies will shock the leaders of the new Axis powers. The Allies must learn to support these internal opposing forces. As we have seen with Afghanistan, Vietnam, and other recent conflicts, the damage that small bands of dedicated counter revolutionaries can inflict with modern weapons is significant. It will become increasingly clear that the general populations of the new Axis powers do not support their leaders' dominance plans as the Allies withdraw from those economies. Read the article "Daughter of Top Putin Ally Alexander Dugin, Who Pushed for Ukraine Invasion, Killed by Car Bomb outside Moscow" from *Fox News*.[110]

5

Physical Weapons and Technologies of World War III

IT IS BEYOND the scope of our discussion here to discuss all the physical weapons and technologies that will be needed to win World War III. But what we can and should discuss are the dual use devices and technologies that can be developed for winning World War III and the war on global warming. Examples of potential dual use physical weapons and technologies are autonomous devices, nuclear energy, nanotechnologies, quantum information sciences and technologies, synthetic biotechnologies and green-based chemicals, brain health care, and civilian-driven nautical flotilla and naval reserves.

Autonomous Devices

Drones developed and manufactured for use in World War III can also be applied to forestry management and agriculture and used to detect and track illegal fishing in the oceans, eliminate invasive animal species, and defeat illegal economies.

Nuclear Energy

The West needs to get back into nuclear energy in a big way. Chinese and Russian designs for nuclear energy plants now dominate the nuclear energy industry. This trend must be reversed, because nuclear energy facilities ultimately make their way to nuclear weapon designs and advancement. For more information, read "Nuclear Power Can Help the Democratic World Achieve Energy Independence" from *Nature*.[111]

Nanotechnologies

Small swarms of everything will make their presence felt on the battlefields during World War III. These technologies will also have multiple consumer applications.

Quantum Information Sciences and Technologies

For information about quantum information sciences and technologies, read "A Huge Step forward in Quantum Computing Was Just Announced: The First-Ever Quantum Circuit" from *Science Alert*.[112]

For additional information on the ideas presented in this chapter, see the following:

- "China, South Korea Racing for Stealth Fighter Supremacy"[113]
- "US Army Sets Timeline for Demo of New, Hard-to-Detect Mobile Command Post"[114]
- "RIMPAC Lessons Will Inform Navy's Pursuit of a Program-of-Record Unmanned Ship in 2025"[115]
- "US Navy Sail toward a Less-Crewed Future"[116]
- "Russia-Ukraine War Catapults Israeli Arms Industry to Global Stage"[117]
- "Northrop Grumman Received $3.29 Billion to Develop a Missile Defense System that Could Protect the Entire U.S. Territory from Ballistic Missiles"[118]
- "Renewable Diesel for Our Changing World"[119]

- "Ukraine's Drone Spotters on Front Lines Wage New Kind of War"[120]
- "ATACMS Replacement: Lockheed Martin Is Developing a New Missile for HIMARS and M270 with a Range of up to 650 km, It Will Be Able to Destroy Ships"[121]
- "Western Tech Continues to Flow into Russia Despite Sanctions: Report"[122]
- "Turkey's Defense Industry Eyes Export Expansion as Government Navigates Geopolitical Stage"[123]
- "Russia Launches Iranian Satellite into Space"[124]
- "New Iran Satellite Presents Significant Challenge to Israel, US and Allies—Experts"[125]
- "Iran to Build 3 More Suspected Spy Satellites as Concern Mounts over Russia Ties"[126]
- "Dozens of IRGC-Linked Flights Landed in Moscow; U.S. Says Drone Deal Advancing"

  Data shows 42 flights by Iranian firms under U.S. sanctions—since Ukraine war began. U.S. official says drone deal moving ahead: "Russians are training in Iran"[127]
- "China Unveils Game-Changing Electronic Warfare Drones"

  China's FH-95 drone is designed to disrupt high-tech enemy networks and adds a new dimension to its drone warfare capabilities.[128]
- "US Navy Injects First-of-Kind Unmanned Experiments into Multinational Exercise"[129]
- "Billions Pour into Bioplastics as Markets Begin Ramping Up"[130]
- "China Allegedly Developed a New 'Flying Submarine' Drone That Could Penetrate Aircraft Carrier Defenses"[131]
- "China, South Korea Clash over THAAD Anti-Missile System"[132]
- "There Is a Profound Disconnect in Battery Metals"[133]
- "The Place with the Most Lithium Is Blowing the Electric-Car Revolution"[134]

- "China Targets Israeli Technology in Quest for Global Dominance as U.S. Frets"[135]
- "Graphene Oxide Membranes Reveal Unusual Behavior of Water at the Nanoscale"[136]
- "New US Marine Regiment Shows Off Capabilities at RIMPAC ahead of Fall Experimentation Blitz"[137]
- "US Goes the 'Hypersonic-Way' to Develop Next-Gen Artillery; Tests 'Air-Breathing' Shells for Its Howitzers"[138]
- "'Bullet Made out of Light': Army to Field First Stryker-Mounted Combat Laser in Next 45 Days"[139]
- "DARPA Selects Companies for Inter-Satellite Laser Communications Project"[140]
- "Army Must Start 'Leaning' on Kinetic Options for Counter-Drone as Autonomous UAS Proliferate"[141]
- "Lockheed Martin's Next Generation Interceptor Hits New Milestone"[142]
- "Watch Lockheed Martin Test Its Layered Laser Defense System"[143]
- "Missile Defense Agency Priorities Include Hypersonics, Guam, Hill Says"[144]
- "Ramjet-Powered Artillery Will Make U.S. Ground Forces More Fearsome Than Ever"[145]
- "US Points New-Gen Missile Defense Radar at China, Russia"[146]
- "DF-26: The Navy Has Plans to Destroy China's Best 'Carrier Killer' Missile"[147]
- "Space Force Takes Over All Military Satellite Communications"[148]
- "War in Ukraine Highlights the Growing Strategic Importance of Private Satellite Companies—Especially in Times of Conflict"[149]
- "Switzerland Will Abandon the American M109 KAWEST Howitzer in Favor of the Swedish Archer or German RCH 155 AGM"[150]

- "Demand Is so High for the Legendary Bayraktar Drones Used to Defend against Russia's Ukraine Invasion That Their Turkish Maker Has a 3-Year Waitlist"[151]
- "SpaceX Gets $1.9 Million Air Force Contract for Starlink Services in Europe and Africa"[152]
- "NATO Member Poland Is Going to Asian Powerhouse to Find a Replacement for Its Aging Soviet-Era Fighter Jets"[153]
- "Air Force Official: We're 'Starting to Lose Our Lead' in Propulsion"[154]
- "In a Show of Strength, the U.S. Has Once Again Tested Its Minuteman III ICBMs"

  > The United States has just completed another successful test fire of a "blank" Minuteman III ICBM missile. The test proves that the missiles are still fit for purpose.[155]

- "Lockheed Delivers High-Energy Laser Four Years in the Making to US Navy"[156]
- "Commercial Geospatial Technologies That Detect GPS Disruptions to Be Tested in Military Exercises"[157]
- "China's Navy Could Have 5 Aircraft Carriers, 10 Ballistic Missile Subs by 2030 Says CSBA Report"[158]
- "Spain Receives First THeMIS Unmanned Ground Vehicle"[159]
- "US Army Digs New Sandbox for Laser Weapons"[160]
- "Lockheed Martin Is the First in the World to Deliver the HELIOS Laser Weapon—It Works on the Principle of the 'Death Star'"[161]
- "China Develops 'Anti-Stealth Radar' so Small That It Could Be Set Up Anywhere, Including Rooftops—Scientists"[162]
- "Inside the Software That Will Become the Next Battle Front in US-China Chip War"[163]
- "Upstart Anduril Australia Hopes to Make 100s of Large Drone Subs, 'ITAR Free,' CEO Says"[164]
- "As DoD Shifts to Smaller Satellites, Rideshare Questions Emerge"[165]

- "Russia's Naval Doctrine May Call for Challenging the West, but Does It Have the Shipyards?"[166]
- "Saudi Arabia Bought the Best American THAAD Air Defense System for $15 billion and Will Prepare Four Sites for Them by 2026"[167]

6

Military Personnel of World War III

IN CHAPTER 3, we learned that the US is stuck in strategic atrophy. We also learned that war and peace coexist—a classic case of yin and yang. Add the fact that both the US Military and civilian society have suffered from self-inflicted woke damage and you can see the declining national recruitment and interest in joining the military.

> The pool of those eligible to join the military continues to shrink, with more young men and women than ever disqualified for obesity, drug use or criminal records. Army Chief of Staff Gen. James McConville testified before Congress that only 23% of Americans ages 17-24 are qualified to serve without a waiver to join. An internal Defense Department survey obtained by NBC News found that only 9% of those young Americans eligible to serve in the military had any inclination to do so.[168]

In my second book, *Reject Self-Serving Power,* I made the following pleas:

Looking at Leadership Through the Lens of the Bottom of the Wealth Inequality Pyramid

My Plea to CEOs, Investors, Boards of Directors, and Senior Management Teams: I understand you all need to target customers that can pay you the most. I understand you must be frugal and manage your expenses. I understand you have a responsibility to your shareholders. I understand you all want the (best) people. I get it. I have been in your shoes. I have been there myself. All I am asking is for you to think about and discuss: Looking at Leadership Through the Lens of the Bottom of the Wealth Inequality Pyramid and to start looking at those people at the bottom of the Pyramid as new customer target markets — not just drains on society. I have forecasted these target markets to approximate $4 Trillion – $8 Trillion annually. (See Book 1.) If you have a new target market opportunity bigger than that, give me a call.

My Plea to the Government Sector: If you have not already done so, please read my Book 1 and study what JM Prophecies Brain Care Corporation is all about. It is time to make our neighborhoods and Country safe and to reform our outrageous prison system. These 2 goals and decisions are NOT mutually exclusive. We can solve both problems together at the same time.

I also discussed at length that in the US, approximately thirty million men of working age are not working. I now make this plea to the US Military: Why not follow your history of leading societal change like your integration of black soldiers into the military? As cited in my second book, the US Marine Corps is currently revisiting its long-term recruitment and retention policies. Let us follow the marines and close the gap between military and civilian populations. Let us use the military to help those who disqualify due to obesity, drug use, or criminal records. Instead of clinging to two-to-six-year terms for initial service, why not offer probationary tryout periods of ninety days, six months, or some other short term? Military families with generations of service are disappearing from the country. Why not start new military families? Why not have a standing reserve of millions or tens of millions under short-term tryouts?

I commend the US Marine Corps for opening a new initiative. Now it is up to civilian organizations to partner with all the branches of the US Military and build on this initiative. For more information, see the articles "Army Opens Its Doors to Recruits Who Fail to Meet Initial Body Fat and Academic Standards amid Recruiting Crisis" from *Military.com* and "Thanks to Leftist Corruption, U.S. Military Recruiting Is in Total Freefall" from *The Federalist*.[169] Also see the following excerpt from the article "Recruitment Is Now a Real Threat to a Frail Force Facing Formidable Foes" from *Breaking Defense*:

> "Under-manned units over-operate, resulting in an unrested and less specialized force. And the only real solution to this issue is to add fresh bodies to the force," writes Mackenzie Eaglen of AEI.[170]

Ending Strategic Atrophy

It is time to inform our citizens that we are in a yin and yang of war and peace. We must defeat the new Axis powers, and that must take precedence over net-zero carbon. For more information, read the articles "The Marines of the Future" from the *Washington Examiner* and "Marines Eying the Overlooked Individual Ready Reserve to Keep Talent" from the *Marine Times*.[171] Also see the following excerpt from the article "Air Force Drag Queen Show Betrays the Military's Mission" from the *American Spectator*:

There are no "safe spaces" on an aircraft carrier or in a submarine. Drag queens who want to embrace their feminine side are no substitute for the warriors "in olive drab" or "in brown khaki." And above all, "Diversity, Equity, and Inclusion" is no substitute for "Duty, Honor, Country."[172]

7

Economic Strategies and Alignments

THE NEW AXIS powers are using supply chains, fossil fuels, and the distant promises of green energy and net-zero carbon as economic weapons and globally collaborated strategies against the Allies and their friends. The US must counter these strategies with its own four-part strategy. First, we must immediately regain our leadership in fossil fuels for our own energy security and the energy security of our allies. This will require a national, political recommitment to the fossil fuel industry that is not short-term. Stop draining the strategic petroleum reserve to artificially reduce inflation for political purposes, and stop selling those reserves to China as cheap oil.

Second, we must restart our commitment to nuclear energy with the goal of becoming the world's leader in nuclear energy and research. Then we can continue advancing green technologies. This will require a significant investment in securing our national energy grid. Allow time for the natural process of capitalism to pick green energy winners and losers. We need millions of iterations and three pendulum swings to eventually pave the road for a successful future in green energy.

In chapter 3 of my second book, I discussed what I call a sea of unforced errors: "Our Country is drowning in a sea of unforced errors: mistakes, wrong decisions, and bad ideas." Top-down green energy is over flowing the sea of unforced errors. Self-appointed elites believe that they know better than millions of real economic data points worked through the global energy marketplace. For more information, see the articles "US Infrastructure Is Nowhere Near Ready for Biden's Electric Vehicle Timeline" from *The Hill*, "Money Won't Solve America's Power Grid Problems" from *Oil Price*, and "Back to the Drawing Board: Reinventing Offshore Wind Turbines" from *TechXplore*.[173]

Finally, we need to begin building the climate change bridge as I set forth in my third book and exporting those strategies to other parts of the world. Imagine the power of implementing the great water opportunity strategy in the Middle East, Sahara, and other deserts of the world.

As a review, my third book, *Building the Climate Change Bridge*, sets forth the following:

Primary Strategies To Build the Climate Change Bridge

TO BE VERY clear, our primary and foundational strategies for building the climate change bridge are to:

1. Transfer ocean salt waters to the deserts of the world in sufficient quantities to build a centuries-long runway to control rising ocean coastlines;
2. Desalinate those transferred salt waters to be used to reverse groundwater and surface fresh water depletion, ultimately increasing the world's usable and available fresh waters to 5 percent of the earth's total water; and
3. Use the infrastructure previously developed to reverse biodiversity loss, desertification, and ocean pollution.

For more information, see the articles "Water Scarcity: EU Countries Forced to Restrict Drinking Water Access" from *Deutsche Welle*; "Sea Level Rise Is Expected to Worsen Coastal Flooding—Even on Sunny Days, According to New NOAA Report" from *ABC News*; and "A New Storm Is Brewing in Struggle over Climate Change: Homeowner's Insurance" from *The Hill*.[174]

Fossil Fuels Are Global Commodities with No Boundaries to Restrict Flows

A fatal flaw in top-down green energy philosophy is the belief that fossil fuels can be controlled by country boundaries. As proven recently, fossil fuels are entirely fluid, free to go from country to country even if restrictions are tried. Restricted US fossil fuels will simply be replaced by other countries, most often driven by the new Axis powers. For more, see the following:

- "Russian Crude Is Quietly Flowing to European Buyers like Italy and Spain as EU Sanctions Loom"[175]
- "Russian Authorities Are Putting the Country's Defense Enterprises on a 24-Hour Work Schedule"[176]
- "How Commodity Traders Are Helping Fund Russia's War"[177]
- "Offshore Drilling Is Coming Back with a Bang"[178]
- "Top Coal Firm in World Cashing in on Global Energy Crisis"[179]
- "An Unknown Chinese Merchant Spends $376 Million on 13 Cargo Ships for Risky Russian Oil Transfers on the High Seas, Report Says"[180]
- "Germany's Painful Lesson for US Climate Warriors on the Dangers of Going Green"[181]

Also see the following excerpt from the article "High-Impact Oil and Gas Drilling Is Back" from *Oil Price*:

- Rystad Energy: So far this year, E&P firms have discovered over 1.7 billion boe at high-impact wells, nearly quadruple the 450 million boe discovered for the whole of 2021.

- Companies plan to drill 33 high-impact wells in 2022, the largest annual number since Rystad Energy started tracking the sector in 2015.
- Latin-America, Africa and the East-Mediterranean are emerging as exploration hotspots.[182]

Oil Refineries

Like their decades-long war on nuclear power, self-serving power zealots of green energy have now won their war against oil refineries in the US. Oil companies no longer invest in US oil refinery projects due to the uncertainty created by the left's war on fossil fuels. Perhaps no other sector of the fossil fuel production chain demonstrates top-down-driven green energy folly more than oil refineries. Stopping the construction of oil refineries in the US will not stop their global construction. It will simply go to other countries dominated by the new Axis powers, ceding more energy leverage and power over the Allies to them. For more information, read the articles "No New Refineries Likely Ever Built Again in the U.S., Chevron CEO Warns" from *Seeking Alpha*; "Global Refining Capacity to Expand with New Projects in Middle East, Asia" from *Oil Price*; and "How a Massive Refinery Shortage Is Contributing to High Gas Prices" from *NPR*.[183]

China's Economic Invasion of the US

China has already started its economic invasion of the US and its allies. Consider the following:

- "We're in an Economic War:' White House, Congress Weigh New Oversight of U.S. Investments in China"[184]
- "Economic Warfare"[185]
- "SEC Adds Alibaba to List of Chinese Companies Facing Delisting"[186]
- "Western Companies in China and Russia Eye Exits"[187]
- "G-7's Infrastructure Plan Offers an Alternative to China's Belt and Road Initiative in a 'Deliberate Way'"[188]

- "China Cuts Tariffs, Cozies up to 16 of World's Poorest Nations with US, Australia Trade Ties Strained"
- China will cut import tariffs on almost all taxable items shipped from 16 of the world's poorest countries, including Cambodia, Laos, Djibouti, Rwanda, and Togo
- China is still smarting from its four-year-old trade dispute with the US, while ties with Australia declined after Canberra called for a probe into the origin of the coronavirus.[189]
- "Why China's Economy Is in Trouble and What It Means for You"
  > Beijing this week slashed interest rates to boost demand after its zero-COVID policy and a property crash rocked the economy.[190]
- "America's Industrial Base Isn't Ready for War with China"
  > Washington must invest immediately in a domestic capacity to build and repair military hardware.[191]

Bringing Manufacturing and Supply Chains back to the US

See the article "U.S. Companies on Pace to Bring Home Record Number of Overseas Jobs" from the Wall Street Journal.[192]

8

Freedom as a Weapon

AS WE DEVELOP our national answer to strategic atrophy, we need to weave in the use of freedom as a weapon against the new Axis powers. Iraq's newfound freedom against the political ideology of Iran is a great example. Putin invaded Ukraine because Ukraine's freedom was undermining his regime. China welched on its agreement to the people of Hong Kong because their freedom was a threat to all of China. China wants to squash Taiwan because of Taiwan's commitment to democracy and freedom.

But freedom is not just a political concept. It is a basic construct of the entire physical world. Freedom is mental and physical. Consider the following:

> Freedom is our Founding Fathers' greatest gift. The physics of freedom should give us a new appreciation of the Founding Fathers.[193]

Examples of how we could use freedom as a weapon against the new Axis powers include publishing articles and giving speeches on what life could be like for countries after their dictators of each are gone. We should appeal directly to the people of those countries and ask:

- What will Russia be like after Putin?
- What will China be like after Xi and the CCP?
- What would a reunified and democratic Korean Peninsula look like?
- What would a democratic Iran look like with unlimited freshwater supplies led by the US Army Corps of Engineers?

We should also support dissident groups in countries belonging to the new Axis powers and their friends. We must continue to support Ukraine until the end of their conflict with Russia. This is a great and historic opportunity to permanently weaken the new Axis powers. There is an important lesson here. When a member of the new Axis powers makes a mistake, the Allies must exploit that mistake until its end.

Another example of how we could use freedom as a weapon against the new Axis powers is opening geographic locations near their countries and the countries of their friends, actively recruiting those citizens into freedom. For example, open a site at Guantanamo Bay Naval Base in Cuba, or build climate change islands as set forth in my second book. These islands would add to the Hawaiian Islands, Midway Island, and Wake Island. The Midway Island and Wake Island would then be added to the state of Hawaii. We should also consider adding Guam and other Pacific American territories to the Hawaiian Islands. US citizenship should be offered to any Pacific Island citizens who lose their islands to rising oceans. I suggest offering US citizenship to people in the Pacific who are persecuted by the new Axis powers.

For more information, see the articles "Putin Ally Lukashenko Faces Revolt from Officers against Ukraine War: Report" from *Newsweek* and "Why Economic Freedom Is More Integral to Foreign Policy than Ever" from the *Washington Examiner*.[194] Also see the following excerpt from the article "China Arrests Cardinal Zen and Religious Freedom Now Faces a Grim Future in Hong Kong" from *Fox News*: "Cardinal Zen's arrest signals that religious freedom in Hong Kong in danger from China."[195]

9

Global Demographics

IT IS NO secret that the industrialized nations are experiencing falling birth rates and populations. I discussed this topic in depth in chapter 16 of my second book. If you have not read this chapter, you should do so. In chapter 24 of my second book, I listed my prophecies for the twenty-first century: "Prophecy Number 1: The population of China and the United States will crisscross at approximately 650 million people."

China's birth rate, marriage rate, and population are in freefall. They are aging at an incredible rate. I also forecasted that China will decline into a balkanized group of states as the ratio between their working-age adults and retirees approaches 1:1 in the twenty-first century. Russia, Iran, and North Korea are in similar demographics. In my second book, I explained that it takes around one hundred years for all totalitarian and socialist societies to collapse. All the new Axis powers are on track to coincide with this historical trend. We need to get out of China before its balkanization begins. For more information, see this excerpt from the article "The Bursting Chinese

Housing Bubble Compounds Beijing's Economic Woes" from the *Wall Street Journal*:

> Home sales and prices are dropping in many cities across the country after rising for years, and the damage is spreading.[196]

10

Top-Down Ideology and Self-Serving Power at Home

UNFORTUNATELY THE NEW Axis powers do not have sole claim to top-down, left-wing ideology. It also continues to thrive in the US and their allied countries. The cancelation of the Keystone XL pipeline started the green energy ideologues' war on fossil fuels and led to economic demise around the world.

Russia's invasion of Ukraine answered any remaining questions about the economic repercussions of green energy policies that also seek to destroy the fossil fuel industries. The top-down, left-wing, green energy crowd has hijacked the green energy movement to advance their own wealth and self-serving power. This hijacking is extremely unfortunate. Global warming is real. Climate change is real. But as I discuss in my third book, *Building the Climate Change Bridge*, we must approach these challenges with cool heads and discipline. Fortunately, as I discuss in my first book, democratic countries live under the three pendulums of society. The pendulums for green energy and fossil fuels are swinging wildly in all directions. Eventually these swings will stabilize, disclosing rational, long-term strategies.

Educating the World about Global Warming and Climate Change

Most people do not understand climate change and global warming. They are not educated in what is still a relatively new field of study. It is akin to our grandparents being thrown into the internet without advance training. One of the key tenets of top-down, left-wing ideology is to keep the citizens ignorant. It is far easier to control citizens' minds if they are kept dumb and in chaos. We need to build a core curriculum for climate change and global warming that is offered to all citizens.

The people are simply not sufficiently informed to make the right decisions. For example, the current message is that we need net-zero carbon by 2050 or the world will come to an end. But that is all conjecture. Do advocates say ocean levels will stop rising in 2050 if net-zero carbon is met? No, they do not dare make such claims. Due to the thermal expansion of oceans and the depletion of groundwaters, ocean levels will not stop rising, even if net-zero carbon is achieved by 2050. Do they say biodiversity loss will stop in 2050 if net-zero carbon is met? No. Only approximately 20 percent of biodiversity loss is due to climate change associated with global warming. Do they say pollution of the oceans will stop in 2050 if net-zero carbon is met? No, because there is very little correlation. See my third book for detailed discussions on these topics.

In summary, it is no wonder why people are frustrated, angry, and lashing out about climate change and global warming. We must begin a national training program that is not driven by self-serving power zealots who have more in common with the new Axis powers than they do with the citizens they are supposed to represent. For more information, see the following:

- "Inside TikTok's Army of Lobbyists of Ex-Senators, Congressmen, and Staffers"[197]
- "Why Pretend Green Pork Will Stop Climate Change?"[198]
- "An Inconvenient Truth: ESG Is Fueling Inflation Woes"[199]

- "What if They Gave a War and Everybody Was Woke?"[200]
- "Gen Zers Turn to TikTok with Their Fantasies of Taking over Corporate America: 'Bring on the 4-Day Workweeks and 6-Hour Days'"[201]
- "Manchin's Mountain Valley Pipeline Dream"[202]
- "'Dirty Ol' Coal' Is Making a Comeback and Consumption Is Expected to Return to 2013's Record Levels"[203]
- "The U.S. Made a Breakthrough Battery Discovery—Then Gave the Technology to China"[204]
- "Exclusive: Missouri Attorney General Investigates Morningstar over ESG Ratings"[205]
- "Climate Change Proposals Putting American Food Supply at Risk, Says Dairy Farmer"[206]
- "Gaslighting: How the Mainstream Media Tries to Drive You to the Left"[207]
- "LA Times Urges Biden to Use Executive Powers to Declare a 'National Climate Emergency'"[208]
- "Senate Passes Inflation Reduction Act after All-Night Vote Series"
  "The Inflation Reduction Act that this Senate Democratic Majority has passed … is the boldest climate package in U.S. history," Senate Majority Leader Chuck Schumer (D-NY) said in a tweet.[209]
- "Tilting at Climate Windmills"[210]
- "Democrats' Inflation Reduction Act is 'economic malpractice': Economist"[211]
- "China Criticizes US Chip Law as Threat to Trade"[212]

Self-serving leftists use green energy speak as a Trojan horse to advance their own agendas. For an example, see the article "Tax and Climate Bill Could Massively Expand IRS Union, Which Almost Exclusively Donates to Democrats" from *Fox News*.[213] Manipulation of the US strategic petroleum reserve for political cover only serves the new Axis powers. See the following from "Asia Gobbles up Cheap U.S. Crude at OPEC's Expense" from *Oil Price*:

- Cheap U.S. oil is increasingly competing with Middle Eastern grades on the spot market.
- Asian buyers have bought some 16 million barrels of U.S. crude on the spot market so far this month.[214]

Also see the excerpt from the article "China's Imports of US Oil Have Hit an 18-Month High as It Pivots away from Russian Crude" from *Markets Insider*:

> US oil is trading at a marked discount to Brent crude, causing American exports to surge.[215]

Inflation and Stagflation—Left-Wing, Green Energy, Economic Ideology and Strategy

See the following:

- "Biden's Created Our Bad New Normal, and He's Loving It"[216]
- "Green Groups Gear up for Next Climate Fight as Historic Bill Clears Congress"[217]
- "'Shocked and Disheartened': How Coal Country Is Reacting to Manchin's Climate Deal"[218]
- "JPMorgan CEO Jamie Dimon: 'Why Can't We Get It through Our Thick Skulls?' America Boosting Oil and Gas Production Is 'Not Against' Climate Change"[219]
- "China Gets a Great Leap Forward from Congress"[220]
- "Bold bill or terrible tax hike? Biden and GOP fight to define new spending law."[221]
- "Biden Officials Push Electric Cars on Recession-Weary Americans from Their 'Policy Fantasyland': Expert"
    > The Heritage Foundation president says the Biden admin's push to switch Americans to electric vehicles amid high energy costs is out of touch.[222]

11

Water, Ocean Pollution, and Natural Resources

OUR PREVIOUS DISCUSSIONS—INCLUDING those in my second and third books regarding the use of fossil fuels and energy as weapons—are not the only parts to this strategy. We must also begin the discussion of what life will be like after the depletion of natural resources and raw materials of all kinds. This takes the green energy discussion to a new level, but perhaps that is precisely what we need to do. We need to be able to say to the new Axis powers, "Weaponizing fossil fuels is so yesterday! We have that covered with our newly embraced plan to transition from fossil fuels to green energy. We also have this great plan to embrace the water opportunity enabled by global warming and increase the world's usable freshwater supplies ten times to 5 percent of the world's water. We have a long-term solution, and new industries are being formed to end the drilling, mining, and gathering of all raw materials. Do you have that?" See the article "'Elephant in the Room': Clean Energy's Need for Unsustainable Minerals" from *Ars Technica*.[223]

EVs' Cattle Stampede Rush to the Raw Materials Cliff

The green energy push to electric vehicles (EVs) is herding the Allies over a raw materials cliff. China has been diligent in securing most of the raw materials needed for an EV industry. Consider the following published by the National Library of Medicine:

> As electric vehicles become more widespread, the demand for special raw materials for the vehicles and, in for the batteries will continue to grow.[224]

So Let Me Get This Straight

No one really knows if enough raw materials exist to convert from internal combustion engines to an EV industry or if they can be used. This stampede is occurring without the benefits of incremental evolution naturally brought on by open capitalism. Even if sufficient raw materials exist and can be used, China has already secured a dominant position that is sufficient to dictate the Allies. Cobalt basically comes from only the Congo. No wonder the Chinese are all over the Congo. This does not even take into consideration the use of child slave labor. But if anyone knows how to exploit slave labor to sell stuff to the West, just ask the CCP.

No one has really compared the total carbon emissions and other polluting emissions from the production and operation of EVs to those from internal combustion engines. How can anyone possibly know? This is the kind of question that would normally get answered in incremental capitalism. But this is not happening in the EV cattle stampede.

China already has a stranglehold on EV and solar energy parts and production. Xi and the CCP must constantly ask themselves how they could have gotten so lucky with the green energy movement placing them in such a position. See the following:

- "How China Dominates the Electric Vehicle Supply Chain"
  When it comes to the massive batteries that are essential to electric vehicles, China is way ahead. It controls something

like three-quarters of the market for the raw materials that go into these batteries, like lithium, cobalt, and nickel. So automakers rely on China for these minerals.[225]

- "How China is Cornering the Market for Electric-Car Batteries"

  The West is sleepwalking into a situation where it has traded its old reliance on Middle East oil for dependence on key metals controlled by China. That's a bad trade, says Simon Wilson.[226]

- "China Is Owning the Global Battery Race"

  That could be a problem for the U.S. Electric cars rely on lithium-ion batteries. China produces 76 percent while the U.S. makes only 8 percent.[227]

- "The Key to Electric Cars Is Batteries. One Chinese Firm Dominates the Industry"[228]

- "How China Dominates Global Battery Supply Chain"[229]

- "Chinese Graphite Dominance Threatens Electric Car Ambitions"

  A rise in demand for electric cars is boosting demand for graphite, a key battery component. As battery and car makers try to secure supplies, China's domination of the graphite market has become a problem.[230]

- "China's Solar Panel Supply Chain Domination Cause for Worry: IEA"[231]

- "China Accounts for Nearly Half of the World's Renewable Energy Capacity"[232]

The global elites are already back pedaling on if EVs can ever really replace internal combustion engine vehicles. See this excerpt from the article "World Economic Forum Calls to Reduce Private Vehicles by Eliminating 'Ownership'" from *Fox Business*:

World Economic Forum says steps need to be taken to reduce reliance on critical metals amid green energy push.[233]

**Weaponizing Water—Flipping the War on
Natural Resources in Favor of the Allies**

In my third book, *Building the Climate Change Bridge,* we set forth the
following strategies:

Primary Strategies To Build the Climate Change Bridge

TO BE VERY clear, our primary and foundational
strategies for building the climate change bridge are to:

1. Transfer ocean salt waters to the deserts of the world in
   sufficient quantities to build a centuries-long runway to
   control rising ocean coastlines;
2. Desalinate those transferred salt waters to be used to reverse
   groundwater and surface fresh water depletion, ultimately
   increasing the world's usable and available fresh waters to 5
   percent of the earth's total water; and
3. Use the infrastructure previously developed to reverse
   biodiversity loss, desertification, and ocean pollution.

Once planned in the US, the previous strategies should be used to
work with desert regions of the world. As further set forth in my third
book:

Number of Great Salt Lake equivalents required to utilize all
cubic kilometers of water for rising ocean levels:
- At Salt Lake depth: 4 meters: 35–138
- Two times Salt Lake depth: 8 meters: 18–69
- Four times Salt Lake depth: 16 meters: 9–35

The Allies should use these strategies as a counter weapon, using the
accumulation of freshwater supplies as a freedom and a natural resource
weaponization plan. Imagine assisting Saudi Arabia to build an inland

saltwater sea and freshwater desalination system that also remediates the ocean dead zone in the region. Imagine assisting Iraq, Mexico, Northern Africa, Argentina, and Chile to build inland saltwater seas and freshwater desalination systems that could send freshwater supplies to the entirety of each region.

The economic growth created by these systems would largely eliminate political conflicts and criminal activities in their respective regions. Populations would be too busy prospering and advancing their lives to worry about wars. A single battalion of US Army Corps of Engineers would have more battlefield success and long-term economic and political impact on a region than an entire army of Allies. The Mexican drug cartels would fade into a sad page of criminal history.

The European Union and NATO could also construct a string of desalination plants on all their coastlines to transfer new freshwater supplies across Europe. We are also looking at the feasibility of installing industrial-sized outdoor chillers in glacier areas to reverse glacial melting. For more information, see the following:

- "Drought Threatens Major Rivers in the U.S. and Europe"[234]
- "Water Flow on the Danube Is One-Third of What It Should Be This Time of Year"[235]
- "Rhine River Drops to Record Lows, Restricting Shipping and Exacerbating the European Energy Crisis"[236]
- "Centuries-Old Warnings Emerge from Riverbed as Europe Faces Historic Drought"
    > The "horrifying" boulders are known as "Hungersteine," or "Hunger Stones,". The stone, dating back to a drought in 1616, is once again visible in the dry riverbed.[237]
- "'The Water Wasn't There': Shrinking of Italy's Lake Garda Shocks Tourists"[238]
- "For Advance Drought Warning, Look to the Plants"[239]
- "UN, Experts Warn of Serious Water Problems for Iraq"[240]
- "Facing Drought, Iraq Asks Turkey to Release More Water along Tigris, Euphrates Rivers"[241]

- "Conflicts Exacerbate Drought That Threatens Millions in Syria, Iraq"

  The Syrian regime's extended war on its own people and Iran's river diversions have exacerbated the regional drought, posing a serious threat to food security and the environment. The Middle East drought, which is worsening at an unprecedented pace, presents a serious risk to regional food security and the environment. The lack of rain and decline in river water threaten more than 12 million residents of Syria and Iraq, where the current dry season is the worst in decades. Across the border from Syria, a full 40% of Iraq is now considered a desert area.[242]

- "Egypt to Build Desalination Plant in Iraq"

  Egypt plans to build a desalination plant on the Euphrates River to help address acute water shortages in southern Iraq amid lack of rainfall and poor management of water resources.[243]

- "The World's Rivers Are Drying Up from Extreme Weather. See How 6 Look from Space"[244]

- "China Plans Cloud Seeding to Protect Grain Crop amid Drought"[245]

- "Droughts Hurt World's Largest Economies"[246]

- "Plunging Water Levels of China's Yangtze Reveal Ancient Statues"[247]

Asian Pacific Exporting Economies and Nations Are Destroying the Oceans of the World

For decades, the US sent its manufacturing base to China and the South Pacific, due largely to their significantly lower production costs. Those lower costs were mostly because of the difference in environmental costs. That environmental cost is now being sent to the West. Ironically, the waters of the South China Sea are currently the most militarily contested waters in the world. The US Navy takes great pride in navigating the South China Sea. The sea of unforced errors once again continues to fill.

Xi boasts that the Chinese Navy will soon come to Hawaii. The danger coming to Hawaii from the South China Sea is not the Chinese Navy. The danger to Hawaii is the pollution-ravaged waters from the South China Sea making their way to all the oceans. The world must establish a string of climate change islands around the Central and South Pacific Oceans to "corral" and remediate those polluted waters. See the following:

- "Marine Debris and Ocean Pollution in Hawaii—Plastics Are Becoming a Big Problem"[248]
- "The Looming Environmental Catastrophe in the South China Sea"[249]
- "In Deep Water: Current Threats to the Marine Ecology of the South China Sea"[250]
- "The Environmental Collateral Damage of the South China Sea Conflict"[251]

Ocean Pollution Can Only Be Stopped by Repositioning Our Economy from Central and South Pacific Nations to the Western Hemisphere

Ocean pollution is becoming as important as global warming. Most ocean pollution comes from Central and South Pacific nations. This massive amount of ocean pollution is primarily due to activities related to the production and export of products shipped around the world. It can only be stopped by cutting economic ties and supply chains with these nations and repositioning production to the Western Hemisphere. I discuss this topic in all my books. I will devote an entire book to this subject in the future. For now, consider the following:

- "How Three Companies Are Cleaning up the World's Plastic-Choked Rivers"[252]
- "Which Countries Create the Most Ocean Trash?"[253]
- "China's Ocean Waste Surges 27% in 2018: Ministry"
    China dumped a total of 200.7 million cubic meters of waste into its coastal waters in 2018, a 27% rise on

the previous year. Environmental groups have expressed concern that China, desperate to clean up its own rivers, is dumping increasing amounts of trash in its seas instead.[254]

- "Five Asian Countries Dump More Plastic into Oceans than Anyone Else Combined: How You Can Help"[255]
- "Asia's Rivers Send More Plastic into the Ocean than All Other Continents Combined"[256]
- "Indonesia Is Facing a Plastic Waste Emergency"
  Attempts to reduce the amount of waste flowing into the ocean from Indonesia are having limited success.[257]
- "Why the Global Soil Shortage Threatens Food, Medicine and the Climate"[258]
- "Scientists Say Landfills Release More Planet-Warming Methane than Previously Thought"[259]

The strategy to build climate change islands as set forth in my second book could also be used by the Allies against the new Axis Powers to counter ocean pollution and natural resources and aid freedom. Imagine Galapagos type islands built from ocean pollution and debris off the coasts of Midway Island, Wake Island, Guam, the Caribbean islands, the Korean Peninsula, the Philippines, the Gulf of Mexico, and the Florida Keys. Imagine replicating the Great Barrier Reef in Australia. See "Satellites Show Landfills Releasing Large Amount of Methane" from *VOA News*.[260]

Long-Term End Goal—Building the Infrastructure to Filter All Ocean Waters

Let us increase the percentage of the earth's fresh water available for human use from 0.5 percent to 5 percent. If this goal were achieved, it would imply that we could filter out micro plastic fibers, forever chemicals, and other pollution from all the ocean waters approximately every twenty years. Because of all the toxic materials released into the environment over the centuries, it will eventually become necessary to filter the oceans. For more information, see the following:

- "It's Raining PFAS: Even in Antarctica and on the Tibetan Plateau, Rainwater Is Unsafe to Drink"[261]
- "It's Literally Raining 'Forever Chemicals', and the Storm Could Last for Decades"[262]
- "Scientists Link 'Forever Chemical' Exposure to Development of Liver Cancer"[263]
- "EPA Action Boosts Grassroots Momentum to Reduce Toxic 'Forever Chemicals'"[264]

Long-Term Impact of Green Energy Installations Is Unknown

One of the major ocean pollution unknowns is the long-term impact of green energy installations, including solar and wind installations. Because green energy is being crammed down the world's throat, normal capitalistic free markets are not being given the time to sort through the technology and economic issues. We could easily be making matters worse. Consider the following from "Chinese Green Ambitions' Dirty Side: Beijing Faces Recycling Challenge as Millions of Wind Turbines and Solar Panels near Retirement":

- Contaminated soil, water, and air—not to mention carbon emissions—could be the legacy of old wind and solar equipment without a massive recycling effort.
- Despite being on the government's policy road map, a recycling ecosystem for decommissioned equipment is in its infancy.[265]

Windmill Farms Impact on New England Fisheries

See "Not Green: Offshore Wind 'Industry' Destroying Fishing Grounds, Birds & Marine Life."[266]

Developing a Strategy for Climate Change
Lakes and Islands for Antarctica

Argentina, Chile, Australia, and New Zealand are the closest countries to Antarctica. Research should be done to determine if climate change

lakes and islands could be used to develop a long-term plan for melting glaciers in Antarctica.

Developing a Strategy for Climate Change Lakes and Islands for Afghanistan

I think most people would believe that our nation's involvement in Afghanistan did not go as planned. Perhaps a climate change lake built in Afghanistan with the entire region as partners could achieve what twenty years of military occupation could not. Imagine what might have been if that had been the goal for the last ten years of occupation. Afghanistan would now be a water and climate change model for the world. See the following:

- "Nearly 1 Year After Afghanistan Exit, Gen. Keane Says 'We're Right Back Where We Started' in 2001"
  Keane also slammed President Biden for giving Americans a 'false narrative' of the Afghanistan situation.[267]
- "Afghanistan Shrivels in Worst Drought in Decades"[268]
- "Global Warming and Afghanistan: Drought, Hunger and Thirst Expected to Worsen"[269]
- "In Afghanistan, a Drought Highlights the Climate Crisis"
  A reservoir on the outskirts of Kabul offers a glimpse into the country's past and its possible future.[270]
- "Afghanistan: Hunger and Poverty Surge as Drought Persists"[271]
- "How the Western Drought Is Pushing the Power Grid to the Brink"[272]
- "China Just Ran into Something That Could Be Even More Devastating for Its Supply Chains than COVID-19 Lockdowns: A Record Heat Wave"[273]

12

Peacetime Nuclear Industry Necessary to Stay Ahead in Nuclear Weapons

WHY THE UNITED STATES SHOULD REMAIN ENGAGED ON NUCLEAR POWER: GEOPOLITICAL AND NATIONAL SECURITY CONSIDERATIONS

Nuclear energy has shown much promise and faced considerable challenges since its origins in the mid-20th century. While the United States drove the early charge for safe nuclear power around the globe, its leadership has waned in recent decades. US reactors now under construction—following no orders for such plants in the United States for several decades— have gone well over planned budgets and schedules. And while the United States was once the leading international supplier of reactors, other countries have since stepped forward to fill that role.

Columbia University's Center on Global Energy Policy, as part of its wider work on nuclear energy, is examining the impact of potential American disengagement from nuclear power's development and where opportunities exist to step back in and shape its future. The program also will assess the US nuclear waste management program and efforts to collaborate with other countries on advanced reactor development as well as options for improvement on both fronts. This effort includes a two-part commentary on some of the benefits the United States might derive from increasing its engagement on nuclear power. The first in the series explored the important role nuclear energy can play in lowering air pollution and greenhouse gas emissions to avoid the worst potential outcomes of climate change.

The second part of the series, this piece, examines the geopolitical and national security implications of the United States and its traditional allies effectively ceding the international nuclear energy marketplace to the Chinese and Russians. The nuclear program's ultimate goal is to inform readers—policy makers, industry leaders, academics, and others—with objective, research-based analysis. It will strive in the months and years ahead to contribute constructively to a necessary dialogue on the future of nuclear power.[274]

ENVIRONMENTALISTS AND SELF-SERVING power zealots have virtually destroyed the Allies' nuclear industry and research. Once again, hijacking common sense to gain and retain power won out over the citizens' well-being. They largely did their subversion by passing mountains of regulations and oversight to ensure that no nuclear project could be completed timely or under any cost. Consider the following data points:

- "Russian and Chinese Designs Dominate Nuclear Reactors, Warns IEA Chief"
- Since 2017, 87% of the new reactors which have broken ground are Russian and Chinese designs, IEA Executive Director Fatih Birol said in a statement on Thursday.
- "Advanced economies have lost market leadership," Birol said.
- The IEA has put together a plan for how the world can reach net zero emissions by 2050, and in that plan, the amount of nuclear power generation has to double between 2020 and 2050.[275]
- "U.S. Selects Test Plant for Advanced Nuclear Reactor Fuel"[276]
- "Germany Says It May Leave Its Final 3 Nuclear Energy Plants Running for Longer than Planned, Reversing Nearly a Decade of Work"[277]
- "Japan Fears Putin Will Bring Nuclear Bombs Back to Battlefield"[278]
- "Nuclear Power Plants Are Struggling to Stay Cool"[279]
- "Iran's 'Ambitious' Nuclear Program 'Moving Ahead Very, Very Fast,' Warns IAEA Head"[280]
- "UN Nuclear Chief: Ukraine Nuclear Plant Is 'Out of Control'"[281]
- "France to Curb Nuclear Output as Europe's Energy Crisis Worsens"
    High river temperatures restrict EDF's ability to cool plants.[282]
- "German Chancellor: Germany Could Keep Nuclear Power Plants Operating after All"[283]
- "Nuclear Power Is on the Brink of a $1 Trillion Resurgence, But One Accident Anywhere Could Stop That Momentum"[284]
- "This Tiny Modular Nuclear Reactor Just Got the Green Light from U.S. Regulators"[285]
- "Factbox: Energy Crisis Revives Nuclear Power Plants Globally"[286]
- "Goldman Sachs Doesn't See Nuclear as a Transformational Technology for the Future"[287]
- "Rolls-Royce Working on $300m US Department of Defense Contract to Build Transportable Micro Nuclear Reactor"[288]

- "Inside the Fight over California's Last Nuclear Power Plant"[289]
- "Zaporizhzhia: Real Risk of Nuclear Disaster in Ukraine—Watchdog"[290]
- "Russia Announces Temporary Withdrawal from New START Treaty"[291]
- "Russian Forces Threaten to Blow up Europe's Largest Nuclear Reactor"[292]
- "Why the US Needs Russian Uranium"[293]
- "France Will Spend 10 Billion Euros to Relaunch Nuclear Energy"[294]
- "California and Germany Could Save Nuclear Reactors"[295]
- "How a Florida Nuclear Power Plant Became a Crocodile Nursery

  > For nearly 45 years, crocodiles have called the man-made cooling canals at the Turkey Point Nuclear Plant in Homestead, Florida home.[296]

- "Dow, X-Energy to Drive Carbon Emissions Reductions through Deployment of Advanced Small Modular Nuclear Power

- Dow and X-energy collaborate on intent to provide process heat and power at one of Dow's U.S. Gulf Coast facilities by ~2030.

- Dow is first manufacturer to announce intention to develop small modular nuclear technology options.[297]

- "Russian TV Airs Nuclear Missile Warning for U.S., Britain"[298]
- "Europe's Energy Crisis Has Gotten so Bad That French Power Stations Are Being Allowed to Break Environmental Rules as a Fresh Heatwave Looks Set to Cause More Chaos"[299]
- "US Military 'Furiously' Rewriting Nuclear Deterrence to Address Russia and China, STRATCOM Chief Says"

  > But America's "expertise is just not what it was at the end of the Cold War," warns Adm. Chas Richard. The United States is "furiously" writing a new nuclear deterrence theory that simultaneously faces Russia and China, said the top commander of America's nuclear arsenal—and needs more Americans working on how to prevent nuclear war.

Officials at U.S. Strategic Command have been responding to how threats from Moscow and Beijing have changed this year, said STRATCOM chief Navy Adm. Chas Richard. As Russian forces crossed deep into Ukraine this spring, Richard said he delivered the first-ever real-world commander's assessment on what it was going to take to avoid nuclear war. But China has further complicated the threat, and the admiral made an unusual request to experts assembled at the Space and Missile Defense Symposium in Huntsville, Alabama, on Thursday: "We have to account for three-party [threats]," Richard said. "That is unprecedented in this nation's history. We have never faced two peer nuclear-capable opponents at the same time, who have to be deterred differently." The need for a new deterrence theory comes as institutional expertise on avoiding nuclear war has atrophied, Richard said.[300]

- "Finns Say Yes to Nuclear Waste"
  Finland is building the world's first permanent disposal site for nuclear waste. As Teri Schultz finds, there's no shortage of people wanting to be its neighbors.[301]
- "Russia Threatens to Sabotage European Nuclear Power Plants"[302]
- "Advanced Nuclear"
  New reactors and technologies hold the promise of the future of clean, reliable energy. But the possibilities go well beyond electricity generation. The nuclear reactors of tomorrow—some less than a decade away—will offer a variety of benefits such as water desalination, process heat and alternative fuels generation, and access to power beyond the grid. They will help remote areas have reliable and clean electricity options and provide immediate power after a disaster. Some designs will even allow us to recover and recycle elements in used nuclear fuel that can still produce energy. These reactors are the backbone

of our carbon free future, and an NEI survey of its 19 utility members found that more than 300 new SMRs are planned to be deployed over the next 25 years.[303]

- "US Small Modular Reactor Production Can Begin"[304]
- "Bill Gates-Backed Firm Raises $750M to Develop Small Nuclear Reactors"[305]
- "Solving the Rock-Hard Problem of Nuclear Waste Disposal Finland avoided some of the mistakes made elsewhere and opened its waste repository.[306]

The US Must Build a Robust Nuclear Waste Recycling Industry and Lead the World in This Capability

There is no reason that the US does not lead the world in recycling nuclear waste other than political will. This is an area of immense opportunity and future value. Consider the following:

5 Facts about Spent Nuclear Fuel

Nuclear energy is one of the largest sources of emissions-free power in the world. It generates nearly a fifth of America's electricity and more than half of its clean energy. During this process, it creates spent or used fuel (sometimes incorrectly referred to as nuclear waste). In fact, some in the industry actually consider it a valuable resource.

5 fast facts on used fuel that's generated from nuclear power.

1. Commercial used nuclear fuel is a solid.
   Used fuel refers to the uranium fuel that has been used in a commercial reactor. The fuel is made up of metal fuel rods that contain small ceramic pellets of enriched uranium oxide. The fuel rods are combined into tall assemblies that are then placed into the reactor.

It's a solid when it goes into the reactor and a solid when it comes out.

2. The U.S. generates about 2,000 metric tons of used fuel each year.

   This number may sound like a lot, but it's actually quite small. In fact, the U.S. has produced roughly 83,000 metrics tons of used fuel since the 1950s—and all of it could fit on a single football field at a depth of less than 10 yards.

3. Used fuel is stored at more than 70 sites in 34 U.S. states.

   Commercial used fuel rods are safely and securely stored at 76 reactor or storage sites in 34 states.

   The fuel is either enclosed in steel-lined concrete pools of water or in steel and concrete containers, known as dry storage casks. For the foreseeable future, the fuel can safely stay at these facilities until a permanent disposal solution is determined by the federal government.

4. Used fuel is safely transported across the United States.

   Over the last 55 years, more than 2,500 cask shipments of used fuel have been transported across the United States without any radiological releases to the environment or harm to the public.

   The fuel is shipped in transportation casks that are designed to withstand more than 99 percent of vehicle accidents, including water immersion, impact, punctures and fires.

5. Used fuel can be recycled.

   That's right!

   Used nuclear fuel can be recycled to make new fuel and byproducts.

   More than 90% of its potential energy still remains in the fuel, even after five years of operation in a reactor.

   The United States does not currently recycle used nuclear fuel but foreign countries, such as France, do.

There are also some advanced reactor designs in development that could consume or run on used nuclear fuel in the future.[307]

Also see the articles "Recycling Gives New Purpose to Spent Nuclear Fuel" from *Pacific Northwest National Laboratory*; "The Energy in Nuclear Waste Could Power the U.S. for 100 Years, but the Technology Was Never Commercialized" from *CNBC*; and "What Is Nuclear Waste, and What Do We Do with It?" from *World Nuclear Association*.[308]

13

Prophecies and Serendipity Pools for World War III Strategies and Tactics

IN MY FIRST book, *Prophecy before Vision,* we discussed the importance of establishing our prophecies as the first step in creating a vision for what is coming in the future and establishing that vision through strategic planning. Accordingly, I offer the following prophecies for *Defeating the New Axis Powers.*

All four countries of the new Axis powers will internally collapse during the twenty-first century. They will first collapse economically and then politically. China will break up and follow the same fate as the Soviet Union, becoming balkanized. Russia will continue its break up and experience even more balkanization. North Korea will reunify with South Korea, resulting in a democratic Korean Peninsula. Iran will follow Iraq into a rocky democracy, followed by a more stable democracy over time. Investments and other assets located in countries belonging to the new Axis powers that are owned by other countries will ultimately be deemed worthless, written off by their owners, and abandoned.

In my first book, we also discussed establishing serendipity pools that we can use to confront these things established in our prophecies. I also offer countries belonging to the Allies the following serendipity pools.

The Allies have tried to work with the new Axis powers for decades. But enough is enough. The new Axis powers only return the Allies' generosity and patience with more lies, intimidation, threats, and use of force. It is time to close the iron curtain on Russia, the bamboo curtain on China, and the haters curtains on Iran and North Korea. Closing these curtains should be done through total economic extrications from all countries belonging to the new Axis powers. These extrications should begin immediately and be put in place within the next ten years. The Allies should also lead the world in increasing its available freshwater supplies to 5 percent of the planet's total water, as laid out in chapter 11.

14

JM Prophecies Corporation Defense Business

AT JM PROPHECIES Corporation, we plan to do whatever we can to help the Allies. At a minimum, we plan to help the nation and the world understand the great water opportunity from global warming, as published in my third book. We also plan to help lead the world in increasing available freshwater supplies to at least 5 percent of the planet's total water. Business incubators shall be established in autonomous devices, desalination, and others to be determined. Finally, we plan to help the US Military recruit from the bottom of the wealth inequality pyramid.

15

Case Studies: World War III War Games

THE CASE STUDIES presented in this chapter will help you devise strategies and tactics to win World War III.

Case Study 1: Geopolitics of Climate Change

Topic Introduction

Do you agree with the author that energy policy must consider both climate change and geopolitics? Why or why not? Do you agree with the author that the new Axis powers are more than happy to play along with the West under the pretense of caring about achieving net-zero carbon, while all along weaponizing fossil fuels and raw materials for green energy? Why or why not?

Reader's Topic Analysis

Reader's Conclusions and Recommendations

Case Study 2: Geopolitics of Climate Change

Topic Introduction

Do you agree with the author that defeating the new Axis powers must always take precedent over defeating global warming? Why or why not?

Reader's Topic Analysis

Reader's Conclusions and Recommendations

Case Study 3: World War III

Topic Introduction

Do you agree with the author that World War III has already begun? Why or why not?

Reader's Topic Analysis

Reader's Conclusions and Recommendations

Case Study 4: The New Axis Powers

Topic Introduction

Do you agree with the author that the new Axis powers have been formed? Do you believe these countries coordinate and plot against the US and its allies? Do you agree with the author's definition of the opposing sides? Do you believe that the Allies must battle and defeat the new Axis powers? Why or why not?

Reader's Topic Analysis

Reader's Conclusions and Recommendations

Case Study 5: The New Axis Powers

Topic Introduction

Do you agree with the author that the new Axis powers have weaponized fossil fuels and energy against the Allies? Why or why not?

Reader's Topic Analysis

Reader's Conclusions and Recommendations

Case Study 6: Conventional Warfare

Topic Introduction

Do you believe that conventional warfare no longer works? Why or why not?

Reader's Topic Analysis

Reader's Conclusions and Recommendations

Case Study 7: Strategic Atrophy

Topic Introduction

Do you believe our country suffers from strategic atrophy? Why or why not? Discuss your understanding of strategic atrophy. What strategies would you suggest to solve it?

Reader's Topic Analysis

Reader's Conclusions and Recommendations

Case Study 8: No Longer Such a Thing as War or Peace

Topic Introduction

Do you believe that there is no such thing as war or peace but that both coexist? Why or why not? Do you agree with the author that the new Axis powers render net-zero carbon a useless strategy? Do you believe that ESG Investing based on carbon emissions is useless?

Reader's Topic Analysis

Reader's Conclusions and Recommendations

Case Study 9: World War III Geographic Theaters

Topic Introduction

Do you agree with the author's discussions of World War III geographic theaters? Why or why not?

Reader's Topic Analysis

Reader's Conclusions and Recommendations

Case Study 10: World War III Geographic Theaters

Topic Introduction

Do you agree with the author that the US needs to continue to expand its global base readiness, not reduce it? Why or why not?

Reader's Topic Analysis

Reader's Conclusions and Recommendations

Case Study 11: World War III Geographic Theaters

Topic Introduction

Do you agree with the author that climate change lakes and islands can serve to expand World War III battlefields in favor of the Allies? Why or why not?

Reader's Topic Analysis

Reader's Conclusions and Recommendations

Case Study 12: Nuclear Power

Topic Introduction

Do you agree with the author that the West needs to get back into nuclear energy in a big way? Why or why not?

Reader's Topic Analysis

____

Reader's Conclusions and Recommendations

____

Case Study 13: Nuclear Power

Topic Introduction

Do you agree with the author that nuclear energy facilities ultimately make nuclear weapon designs and advancements? Why or why not?

Reader's Topic Analysis

____

Reader's Conclusions and Recommendations

____

Case Study 14: Military Personnel Recruiting

Topic Introduction

Do you agree with the author that the military should lead in recruiting practices to start new military families? Why or why not? Do you agree that the military should have a standing reserve of millions or tens of millions under short-term service and should recruit those millions from the bottom of the wealth inequality pyramid? Why or why not?

Reader's Topic Analysis

Reader's Conclusions and Recommendations

Case Study 15: Economic Strategies and Alignments

Topic Introduction

Do you agree with the author's assessments of economic strategies and alignments in chapter 7? Why or why not?

Reader's Topic Analysis

Reader's Conclusions and Recommendations

Case Study 16: Freedom as a Weapon

Topic Introduction

Do you agree with the author's assessments and recommendations for using freedom as a weapon in chapter 8? Why or why not?

Reader's Topic Analysis

Reader's Conclusions and Recommendations

Case Study 17: Global Demographics

Topic Introduction

Do you agree with the author's discussions and prophecies of China's demographics in chapter 9? Why or why not?

Reader's Topic Analysis

Reader's Conclusions and Recommendations

Case Study 18: Left-Wing Green Energy Ideology

Topic Introduction

Do you agree with the author that the left-wing green energy crowd has hijacked the green energy movement to advance their wealth and self-serving power? Why or why not?

Reader's Topic Analysis

Reader's Conclusions and Recommendations

Case Study 19: Left-Wing Green Energy Ideology

Topic Introduction

Do you agree with the author that the green energy and fossil fuels pendulums are swinging wildly in all directions but that eventually these swings will stabilize? Why or why not?

Reader's Topic Analysis

Reader's Conclusions and Recommendations

Case Study 20: Net-Zero Carbon Goals and Outcomes

Topic Introduction

Do you agree with the author's discussion in chapter 10 regarding educating the world about global warming and climate change? Explain why or why not, specifically discussing net-zero carbon.

Reader's Topic Analysis

Reader's Conclusions and Recommendations

Case Study 21: Prophecies for World War III

Topic Introduction

Do you agree with the author's prophecies for World War III as discussed in chapter 13? Why or why not?

Reader's Topic Analysis

Reader's Conclusions and Recommendations

Case Study 22: Prophecies for World War III

Topic Introduction

What additional prophecies would you make for World War III?

Reader's Topic Analysis

Reader's Conclusions and Recommendations

Case Study 23: Serendipity Pools for World War III

Topic Introduction

Do you agree with the author's serendipity pools for World War III as discussed in chapter 13? Why or why not?

Reader's Topic Analysis

Reader's Conclusions and Recommendations

Case Study 24: Serendipity Pools for World War III

Topic Introduction

What different serendipity pools would you make for World War III?

Reader's Topic Analysis

Reader's Conclusions and Recommendations

Case Study 25: JM Prophecies Corporation Defense Business

Topic Introduction

Please prepare a SWOT analysis of the JM Prophecies Corporation defense business as discussed in chapter 14.

Reader's Topic Analysis

Reader's Conclusions and Recommendations

NOTES

Introduction

- *Defeating the New Axis Powers* is the second of a three-part series.
- Defeating the new Axis powers must always take precedent over defeating global warming.

Chapter 1

- World War III has already started.

Chapter 2

- The new Axis powers include China, Russia, Iran, and North Korea
- Weaponize energy with fossil fuels at the tip of the spear
- Russia's invasion of Ukraine has changed everything
- The new Axis powers and friends survive on illegal economies and activities

Chapter 3

- Conventional warfare fought in the twentieth century no longer works in the twenty-first century

- The age of durable disorder
- Our country suffers from strategic atrophy
- There is no such thing as war or peace—both coexist
- All major US policy decisions must be made through the lens of the ongoing coexistence of war and peace
- The new Axis powers render net-zero carbon as a useless strategy, and ESG investing based on carbon emissions is also useless
- Our people do not yet understand that we live in a world where war and peace coexist

Chapter 4

- The new Axis powers are trying to establish new geographic theaters for World War III in order to spread the US and force us to respond
- The US needs to continue to expand its global base readiness, not reduce it
- Forward military base readiness in the Pacific theaters
- Climate change lakes islands can expand World War III battlefields in favor of the Allies

Chapter 5

- Autonomous devices
- The West needs to get back into nuclear energy in a big way; Chinese and Russian designs for nuclear energy plants now dominate the nuclear energy industry
- Small swarms of everything will make their presence felt on World War III battlefields.

Chapter 6

- Declining national recruitment and interest in joining the military
- Why not follow the military's history of leading societal change?

- Why not start new military families?
- Why not have a standing reserve of millions or tens of millions under short-term tryouts?
- Ending strategic atrophy

Chapter 7

- The US must counter the new Axis powers' strategies with its own four-part strategy:
    - Immediately regain our leadership in fossil fuels
    - Become the world's leader in nuclear energy and research
    - Continue advancing green technologies; this will require significant investment in securing our national energy grid
    - Begin building the climate change bridge
- China's economic invasion of the US

Chapter 8

- We need to use freedom as a weapon against the new Axis powers
- Freedom is a basic construct of the entire physical world
- Open geographic locations near countries belonging the new Axis powers and their friends to actively recruit their citizens into freedom.

Chapter 9

- Chapter 16 of my second book: Why are we still doing business with China?
- Chapter 24 of my second book: my prophecies for the twenty-first century. Prophecy number 1: the population of China and the United States will crisscross at approximately 650 million people

Chapter 10

- The left-wing green energy crowd has hijacked the green energy movement to advance their own wealth and self-serving power
- Educating the world about global warming and climate change

Chapter 11

- We must discuss what will life be like after the depletion of natural resources and raw materials of all kinds
- EV's cattle stampede to the raw materials cliff
- So let me get this straight
- Primary strategies to build the climate change bridge
  - Transfer ocean water to the deserts of the world in sufficient quantities to build a centuries-long runway to control rising ocean coastlines
    - Desalinate those transferred waters to reverse groundwater and surface fresh water depletion, and ultimately increase the world's usable fresh waters to 5 percent of the earth's total water (an increase of ten times)
  - Use the infrastructure to reverse biodiversity loss, desertification, and ocean pollution
- Number of Great Salt Lake equivalents required to utilize all cubic kilometers of water to rise ocean levels:
  - At Salt Lake depth: 4 meters: 35–138
  - Two times Salt Lake depth: 8 meters: 18–69
  - Four times Salt Lake depth: 16 meters: 9–35
- The Allies should use these strategies as a counter weapon, using the accumulation of freshwater supplies as a weaponization plan for both freedom and natural resources.

Chapter 12

- Why the United States should remain engaged in nuclear power: geopolitical and national security considerations
- Environmentalists and self-serving power zealots have virtually destroyed the Allies' nuclear industry and research.

Chapter 13

- Prophecies for defeating the new Axis powers
- The Allies' serendipity pools

Chapter 14

- Help the nation and the world understand the great water opportunity from global warming.
- Help the US Military recruit from the bottom of the wealth inequality pyramid.

Preview

The Two $20 Trillion Opportunities

PART 3 OF BUILDING THE CLIMATE CHANGE BRIDGE SERIES

PLANNING THE SELFLESS ECONOMY

FIXING OUR FINANCIAL MESS

The Two $20 Trillion Opportunities focuses on paying for climate change and preparing for *The Selfless Economy*.

Preview

The Leadership Broadcasting Company

A NEW ERA IN MEDIA, NEWS, AND INFORMATION TO CREATE TRUST AND REBUILD THE COUNTRY

The Leadership Broadcasting Company will launch the JM Prophecies Corporation's media company.

Preview

Integrating the Economies of the Western Hemisphere

Integrating the Economies of the Western Hemisphere will begin to build the serendipity pools and strategies for how we can finally integrate the economies of the Western Hemisphere for the advancement of all countries.

Exhibits

Book 1, Book 2, and Book 3 Case Studies

Exhibits for *Prophecy before Vision*
Case Studies: Learning Prophecy

Case Study 1: Criminal Churn

Topic Introduction

The US criminal churn rate approximates seventeen times annually. This level of repeating offenders is over whelming our judicial system. As a result, judges, prosecutors, and politicians turn to ever-lenient prosecutorial strategies to lessen their caseloads. How can the churn rate best be reduced?

Reader's Topic Analysis

____

Reader's Conclusions and Recommendations

____

Case Study 2: Defunding the Police

Topic Introduction

Defunding the police is a topic of great debate. Using the data points presented in prior chapters, please argue both sides: yes, defund the police, or no, defunding the police is a detrimental concept and will only make matters worse.

Reader's Topic Analysis

____

Reader's Conclusions and Recommendations

____

Case Study 3: Mental Illness

Topic Introduction

During the past several years, the trend has been to close traditional mental health care hospitals and institutions. This trend has arguably led to massive numbers of cases where mental illness is not diagnosed or treated. Please provide your analysis of where the country lies as related to mental health care, and also provide any recommendations you may have.

Reader's Topic Analysis

____

Reader's Conclusions and Recommendations

____

Case Study 4: Drug Addiction

Topic Introduction

Imagine you are the parent of a twenty-year-old son. He started using drugs at the age of fifteen. Prior to that time, he was a great student, had many friends, and was admired by his younger brother and sister. He has now been a drug addict for five years. He dropped out of high school and has stolen from you many times to feed his addiction. He has been in and out of rehabilitation four times, each time coming out "clean" but slipping back into addiction. You still love your son, but you and his siblings can no longer believe he will ever get clean. In truth, knowing you all expect him to fail is part of his repeated failures.

Now imagine you are in front of the judge, hearing your son's case for stealing to feed his drug habit. The judge has just informed you of the facilities at JM Prophecies Brain Care. The judge asks your opinions regarding what sentence he should levy on your again convicted son. What would you recommend?

Reader's Topic Analysis

Reader's Conclusions and Recommendations

Case Study 5: Homelessness

Topic Introduction

You are a long-time owner of a beach-front house that you love. You paid $2 million for your house ten years ago. You had it appraised for refinancing two years ago and owe $4 million on a house that appraised for $6 million. An encampment of approximately 300 homeless people now surrounds your house, practically forcing you into staying inside. You no longer have access to the beach without walking through the encampment. A judge recently ruled that the local police can move the encampment but only if they can be moved to suitable housing.

Imagine your city council is meeting that very night, and you have been asked by your neighborhood watch group to testify. What would you say?

Reader's Topic Analysis

Reader's Conclusions and Recommendations

Case Study 6: Neighborhood Gangs Recruiting Your Children

Topic Introduction

Your son and daughter are both good high school students and never get into trouble. Over the last year, two competing criminal gangs have been recruiting both children to join their gangs or face dire consequences. Both gangs are also recruiting your younger elementary-school-aged children, further threatening your older children in their overall recruitment of all your children. The leaders of both gangs and most members were recently arrested and convicted of multiple crimes. The sentence hearing will be held next week, and the prosecutors have asked you to testify. What would you say?

Reader's Topic Analysis

____

Reader's Conclusions and Recommendations

____

Case Study 7: Prisoners' Futures

Topic Introduction

ou have been in prison for ten years. You are up for parole. If paroled, you can leave the prison under oversight of a probation officer. You will have no job and nowhere to go. The parole board offers you the choice of staying in prison in one of JM Prophecies Brain Care's concentric villages of squares or going free onto the street. What would you ask for the board to clarify about JM Prophecies Brain Care, and what would you do?

Reader's Topic Analysis

____

Reader's Conclusions and Recommendations

____

Case Study 8: Prisoner's Family Members

Topic Introduction

You are the wife of a man currently in prison. He has been in prison for five years and has five more years to serve. His prison has entered into an agreement with JM Prophecies Brain Care. You and your children will have the opportunity to move into one of the JM Prophecies Brain Care's villages. What would you ask about JM Prophecies Brain Care, and what would you do?

Reader's Topic Analysis

Reader's Conclusions and Recommendations

Case Study 9: Entrepreneurs Relocating into a JM Prophecies Brain Care Village

Topic Introduction

You are an entrepreneur. You have identified a company you would like to purchase and become the CEO of, but you need external financing to complete the transaction. An affiliate of JM Prophecies has agreed to finance your acquisition with the requirement that you locate the company in a JM Prophecies set of concentric villages, which would place you and your employees next to a prison. What would you do?

Reader's Topic Analysis

Reader's Conclusions and Recommendations

Case Study 10: CEO Prophecy

Topic Introduction

You have read *Prophecy before Vision* and understand its power. What are your type I prophecies? What are your type II prophecies? How do you plan to publish your prophecies with your investors and board of directors? How will you articulate your updated vision to your employees?

Reader's Topic Analysis

Reader's Conclusions and Recommendations

Case Study 11: ESG Fund Manager

Topic Introduction

You have read *Prophecy before Vision* and understand its power. How will your Prophecies alter your investment strategies if at all?

Reader's Topic Analysis

Reader's Conclusions and Recommendations

Case Study 12: CEO—the Technologies of the Times

Topic Introduction

What do you consider to be the technologies of the times? How do you plan for them in your organization?

Reader's Topic Analysis

Reader's Conclusions and Recommendations

Case Study 13: CEO Prophecy—Three Pendulum Fissures

Topic Introduction

Do you believe there are any material fissures in the three pendulums of a society that will impact your organization? If yes, what are they?

Reader's Topic Analysis

Reader's Conclusions and Recommendations

Case Study 14: CEO Prophecy—Serendipity Pools

Topic Introduction

You are the CEO of an international trading company. What serendipity pools and strategy are you planning to recommend to your senior management team?

Reader's Topic Analysis

Reader's Conclusions and Recommendations

Case Study 15: Marketing Senior Vice President—Prophecy

Topic Introduction

You have read *Prophecy before Vision* and understand its power. Your CEO has published his prophecies and has asked how do you look at them from a marketing perspective? How will you articulate your thoughts to your CEO?

Reader's Topic Analysis

Reader's Conclusions and Recommendations

Case Study 16: CEO and Board of Directors—Prophecy for China

Topic Introduction

At your collective strategy, decision, and direction, your Company has made a big bet investing in China. You obviously disagree with JM Prophecies' strategy and James Michael Matthew's first and fourth prophecies. Why do you disagree? What will happen to your company if you bet wrong?

Reader's Topic Analysis

Reader's Conclusions and Recommendations

Case Study 17: CEO and Board of Directors— Prophecy for Green Energy Economy

Topic Introduction

How do you see the conversion of an economy based on fossil fuel energy to one based on green energy playing out in the US and globally? What serendipity pools have you positioned for the coming of a green energy economy? What bets are you considering for pendulum swings created by the conversion? How are you positioning your company on the inside of the pendulum?

Reader's Topic Analysis

____

Reader's Conclusions and Recommendations

____

Case Study 18: CEO and Board of Directors—Prophecy—Aging Populations

Topic Introduction

Have you published any prophecies regarding the aging of populations? If yes, what are they and why did you pick them? If no, why not?

Reader's Topic Analysis

____

Reader's Conclusions and Recommendations

____

Case Study 19: CEO and Board of Directors—Prophecy—Studying and Analyzing Global Demographics

Topic Introduction

Does your company have an established methodology and forecasting policy for monitoring, analyzing, and forecasting global demographics? If no, why not? If yes, what are they? Do you maintain an actuarial chain-link historical forecasting model? If no, why not? If yes, how accurate has it been in predicting the future?

Reader's Topic Analysis

____

Reader's Conclusions and Recommendations

Case Study 20: CEO and Board of Directors—Prophecy—Things to Come

Topic Introduction

Have you published a list of "things to come" actions that you plan to take to alter the future? If yes, what are they? If no, why not? Do you believe you should reconsider?

Reader's Topic Analysis

Reader's Conclusions and Recommendations

Case Study 21: CEO and Board of Directors—Prophecy—Serendipity Pools

Topic Introduction

Have you ever discussed the concept of serendipity pools in any board meetings? If no, would you or should you? Why or why not?

Reader's Topic Analysis

Reader's Conclusions and Recommendations

Case Study 22: CEO and Board of Directors—Prophecy—A Higher Power

Topic Introduction

Have you ever discussed the concept of a higher power in any board meetings? If no, would you or should you? Why or why not?

Reader's Topic Analysis

___

Reader's Conclusions and Recommendations

___

Case Study 23: CEO and Board of Directors—Prophecy—Technologies of the Times

Topic Introduction

Have you published a list of the technologies of the times? If no, why not? If yes, what does the list look like?

Reader's Topic Analysis

___

Reader's Conclusions and Recommendations

___

Case Study 24: CEO and Board of Directors—Prophecy—Swings in the Civil Society Pendulum

Topic Introduction

Do you analyze and make predictions for the swings in the civil society pendulum? If no, why not? If yes, what would such a list of predictions look like?

Reader's Topic Analysis

Reader's Conclusions and Recommendations

Case Study 25: CEO and Board of Directors—*Prophecy before Vision*

Topic Introduction

After reading and studying *Prophecy before Vision*, do you believe it is possible for you to see and predict the future? Do you believe that there are "events to happen" as described in the book, that these events will happen, and that nothing can be done to change or prevent them? Do you believe that you can alter the future through the concept of "things to come"? Do you believe you and your people can always be the smartest people in the room? Do you believe you can make the right decision every time, with only 10 percent of the information? Do you believe there are signs from a higher power to guide you if you act for the good? For each of these questions, please explain why or why not. If you said yes, would you always have said yes?

Reader's Topic Analysis

Reader's Conclusions and Recommendations

Exhibits for *Reject Self-Serving Power Case Studies: Helping Others Be Successful*

Case Study 1: Doing Business in China

Topic Introduction

You are the chair of a publicly traded company that is listed and actively traded on a US stock exchange. You recently read a book documenting the scrutiny and legal and criminal liability incurred by large Japanese companies after World War II. You also read the one hundredth anniversary threat made to the world by the Chinese Communist Party. Your company recently made a large investment in China. What are you thinking, and what should you do? Would your answer change if China invaded Taiwan and/or launched a nuclear attack on Japan?

Reader's Topic Analysis

____

Reader's Conclusions and Recommendations

____

Case Study 2: Doing Business in China

Topic Introduction

Your CPA firm is the independent auditor of the company described in case study 1. You are the engagement partner. You have also read the same materials that the chair has read. What should you do? Has the company included any risk factors dealing with these potential issues in their SEC filings about their operations in China? If yes, what are they? If no, why not? Would your answer change if China invaded Taiwan and/or launched a nuclear attack on Japan?

Reader's Topic Analysis

Reader's Conclusions and Recommendations

Case Study 3: Doing Business in China

Topic Introduction

Your law firm is the lead SEC counsel for the company described in case study 1. You are the engagement partner. You have also read the same materials that the chair has read. What should you do? Has the company included any risk factors dealing with these potential issues in their SEC filings about their operations in China? If yes, what are they? If no, why not? Would your answer change if China invaded Taiwan and/or launched a nuclear attack on Japan?

Reader's Topic Analysis

Reader's Conclusions and Recommendations

Case Study 4: Target Markets at the Bottom of the Wealth Inequality Pyramid

Topic Introduction

You are the owner of a private company in the US. You have read both my first and second book. You are willing to assess whether these could be potential target markets for your company. Where do you begin your assessment?

Reader's Topic Analysis

Reader's Conclusions and Recommendations

Case Study 5: JM Prophecies Brain Care Corporation

Topic Introduction

You are the Governor of a state. Your state is suffering under a wave of crime. You are up for reelection and plan to run for another term. You have read my first and second book and are wondering if the proposals for both prison reform and clearing your state of crime could be viable solutions for you and your state. What should you do? How do you plan to make your initial assessments?

Reader's Topic Analysis

Reader's Conclusions and Recommendations

Case Study 6: JM Prophecies Brain Care Corporation

Topic Introduction

You are the attorney general of a state. Your state is suffering under a wave of crime. You are up for reelection and plan to run for another term. You have read my first and second book and are wondering if the proposals for both prison reform and clearing your state of crime could be viable solutions for you and your state. What should you do? How do you plan to make your initial assessments?

Reader's Topic Analysis

Reader's Conclusions and Recommendations

Case Study 7: JM Prophecies Brain Care Corporation

Topic Introduction

You are the warden of a large state prison. Your prison has a severe inmate aging issue. You have read both my first and second book. You are wondering if the proposal for prison reform as proposed by JM Prophecies Brain Care Corporation could be a viable solution for your prison. What should you do? How do you plan to make your initial assessments?

Reader's Topic Analysis

____

Reader's Conclusions and Recommendations

____

Case Study 8: JM Prophecies Leadership Code

Topic Introduction

You are the CEO of a publicly traded company. You have read the information and understand my discussions of the JM Prophecies leadership code. You are deciding if this leadership approach could be a fit for your company. What are your next steps?

Reader's Topic Analysis

____

Reader's Conclusions and Recommendations

____

Case Study 9: JM Prophecies Leadership Code

Topic Introduction

You are the managing partner of a large investment firm. You have read the information and understand my discussions of the JM Prophecies leadership code. You are deciding if this leadership approach could be a fit for your portfolio companies. What are your next steps?

Reader's Topic Analysis

____

Reader's Conclusions and Recommendations

____

Case Study 10: JM Prophecies Leadership Code

Topic Introduction

You are the founder and sole owner of a private manufacturing company. You have read the information and understand my discussions of the JM Prophecies leadership code. You disagree with my strategies for helping others be successful, instead believing you should make all the important decisions. You have a large bank loan, and the bank has asked if you are familiar with my works. What would you say?

Reader's Topic Analysis

____

Reader's Conclusions and Recommendations

____

Case Study 11: JM Prophecies Leadership Code

Topic Introduction

You are the banker of the company in case study 10. You have read the information and understand my discussions of the JM Prophecies leadership code. You agree with my strategies for helping others be successful, but the CEO and owner disagree. What would you say?

Reader's Topic Analysis

Reader's Conclusions and Recommendations

Case Study 12: Self-Serving Power

Topic Introduction

You are a member of a state legislature. Your family has had a long and successful political career. Your family has always operated with a ruthless, self-serving strategy. Your enemies have been plotting your family's demise. You have read *Reject Self-Serving Power* and want to have an open family discussion about your futures. What should you do and say?

Reader's Topic Analysis

Reader's Conclusions and Recommendations

Case Study 13: JM Prophecies Decision-Making Equation

Topic Introduction

Assume that the same circumstances as case study 12 are true here. What would your JM Prophecies decision-making equation look like?

Reader's Topic Analysis

Reader's Conclusions and Recommendations

Case Study 14: *Rubicon Circles of Power and Time*

Topic Introduction
Assume that the same circumstances as case study 12 are true here. How would you assess your Rubicon circles?

Reader's Topic Analysis

Reader's Conclusions and Recommendations

Case Study 15: Sea of Unforced Errors

Topic Introduction
Assume that the same circumstances as case study 12 are true here. What would your list of past mistakes, wrong decisions, and bad ideas for your family potentially look like? What would the list potentially look like for your enemies?

Reader's Topic Analysis

Reader's Conclusions and Recommendations

Case Study 16: Looking at Leadership through the Lens of the Bottom of the Wealth Inequality Pyramid

Topic Introduction
You are the CEO of a large private company. You have read my plea to look at these target market segments. What would you say and do?

Reader's Topic Analysis

Reader's Conclusions and Recommendations

Case Study 17: Looking at Leadership through the Lens of the Bottom of the Wealth Inequality Pyramid

Topic Introduction

You are the governor of a large state. You have read my plea to look at and study what JM Prophecies Brain Care Corporation is all about. You have also read my assertion that it is time to make our neighborhoods and country safe and to reform our outrageous prison system. You are currently assessing my claim that these two goals are *not* mutually exclusive and that we can solve both problems together at the same time. What are your assessments so far? What further questions do you have?

Reader's Topic Analysis

Reader's Conclusions and Recommendations

Case Study 18: Inequality Economics

Topic Introduction

You are on the staff of the Congressional Budget Office (CBO). You have read my proposal for inequality economics. What do you think?

Reader's Topic Analysis

Reader's Conclusions and Recommendations

Case Study 19: Reindustrialization of the US

Topic Introduction

You are the CEO of a large publicly traded manufacturing company based in the US. You have received an invitation from me to enter into a teaming agreement. What will you do?

Reader's Topic Analysis

Reader's Conclusions and Recommendations

Case Study 20: Circle of Life Retirement Strategy

Topic Introduction

You serve as an advisor to the social security board of trustees. You have read my recommendations for legislative changes to convert linear cliff retirement to a circle of life. What will you tell the board? What do you think they will say?

Reader's Topic Analysis

Reader's Conclusions and Recommendations

Case Study 21: Big Ideas, Quests, and Journeys

Topic Introduction

You serve on the board of a large think tank. You have read my chapter on big ideas, quests, and journeys. Do you have any ideas to bring to the pipeline? If yes, what are they?

Reader's Topic Analysis

Reader's Conclusions and Recommendations

Case Study 22: Integrating Western Hemisphere Economies

Topic Introduction

You are the president of a midsized Latin America Country. You have read my chapter on integrating western hemisphere economies. What are your thoughts?

Reader's Topic Analysis

Reader's Conclusions and Recommendations

Case Study 23: Reversing Time on the US Debt Clock

Topic Introduction

You are on the staff of a state governor, with responsibilities for assessing both your state's and the federal government's budget process. Have you historically used the US debt clock? If yes, how do you use it? If no, why not?

Reader's Topic Analysis

Reader's Conclusions and Recommendations

Case Study 24: It's Not about Race; It's about Leadership

Topic Introduction

You are an alderman for the city of Chicago. You have read my first two books and want to ask me to speak to the city council. What are the areas you want me to discuss?

Reader's Topic Analysis

____

Reader's Conclusions and Recommendations

____

Case Study 25: The Leadership Broadcasting Corporation

Topic Introduction

You are the CEO of a large media company. You have read the preview for my ninth book. What do you think?

Reader's Topic Analysis

____

Reader's Conclusions and Recommendations

____

Exhibits for *Building the Climate Change Bridge Case Studies: Learning How to Build the Climate Change Bridge*

Case Study 1: Net-Zero Carbon

Topic Introduction
Define and discuss your understanding of net-zero carbon.

Reader's Topic Analysis

Reader's Conclusions and Recommendations

Case Study 2: Climate Change Knowledge

Topic Introduction
Define and discuss your understanding of rising ocean coastlines.

Reader's Topic Analysis

Reader's Conclusions and Recommendations

Case Study 3: Climate Change Knowledge

Topic Introduction
Define and discuss your understanding of biodiversity loss.

Reader's Topic Analysis

Reader's Conclusions and Recommendations

Case Study 4: Climate Change Knowledge

Topic Introduction
Define and discuss your understanding of desertification.

Reader's Topic Analysis

Reader's Conclusions and Recommendations

Case Study 5: Climate Change Knowledge

Topic Introduction
Define and discuss your understanding of thermal expansion of the oceans.

Reader's Topic Analysis

Reader's Conclusions and Recommendations

Case Study 6: Climate Change Knowledge

Topic Introduction
Define and discuss your understanding of groundwater and surface fresh water depletion.

Reader's Topic Analysis

Reader's Conclusions and Recommendations

Case Study 7: The Three Pendulums of Energy Policy and Ideology

Topic Introduction

Explain how the three pendulums of energy policy work and how they are changing the evolution of the green energy industry.

Reader's Topic Analysis

Reader's Conclusions and Recommendations

Case Study 8: The New Axis Powers

Topic Introduction

Do you agree with the author's assessment of the new Axis powers and their weaponization of energy? Why or why not?

Reader's Topic Analysis

Reader's Conclusions and Recommendations

Case Study 9: Russia's Invasion of Ukraine

Topic Introduction
Do you believe Russia's invasion of Ukraine has changed the green energy industry and movement? Why or why not?

Reader's Topic Analysis

Reader's Conclusions and Recommendations

Case Study 10: Desalination Industry

Topic Introduction
Define and discuss your understanding of the current state of the desalination industry.

Reader's Topic Analysis

Reader's Conclusions and Recommendations

Case Study 11: Ocean Pollution

Topic Introduction
What do you believe are the most important ocean pollutions to resolve? Why?

Reader's Topic Analysis

Reader's Conclusions and Recommendations

Case Study 12: Energy Economics

Topic Introduction

Please discuss your understanding of how energy policy impacts inflation and global economies.

Reader's Topic Analysis

Reader's Conclusions and Recommendations

Case Study 13: Intergenerational Obligations and Fairness

Topic Introduction

Discuss what you believe are reasonable goals for your generation's obligations and environmental fairness to future generations.

Reader's Topic Analysis

Reader's Conclusions and Recommendations

Case Study 14: US Supreme Court's Decision on EPA Regulations

Topic Introduction

Discuss your understanding of the Supreme Court's decision to restrict the Environmental Protection Agency's power to regulate carbon emissions that cause climate change.

Reader's Topic Analysis

___

Reader's Conclusions and Recommendations

___

Case Study 15: US Supreme Court's Decision on EPA

Topic Introduction

What impact do you believe the Supreme Court's decision on EPA regulations will have on the Securities and Exchange Commission's rules for environmental disclosure or other agencies, such as the USDA?

Reader's Topic Analysis

___

Reader's Conclusions and Recommendations

___

Case Study 16: Green Energy Advocates' Rubicon Circles of Power and Time

Topic Introduction

Explain your understanding of the author's discussion of green energy Rubicon circles of power and time. Do you agree with his assessment? Why or why not?

Reader's Topic Analysis

___

Reader's Conclusions and Recommendations

___

Case Study 17: Globalization

Topic Introduction
Discuss the role of globalization on green energy policy.

Reader's Topic Analysis

Reader's Conclusions and Recommendations

Case Study 18: Globalization

Topic Introduction
Do you agree that globalization is essentially dead? Why or why not?

Reader's Topic Analysis

Reader's Conclusions and Recommendations

Case Study 19: Conclusions, Solutions, and Recommendations

Topic Introduction
Read and discuss chapter 21 of the author's second book, commenting specifically on the author's calculations.

Reader's Topic Analysis

Reader's Conclusions and Recommendations

Case Study 20: Conclusions, Solutions, and Recommendations

Topic Introduction

Do you believe that the author's conclusions, solutions, and recommendations are viable and reasonable to establish future climate change policy upon? Why or why not?

Reader's Topic Analysis

____

Reader's Conclusions and Recommendations

____

Case Study 21: Conclusions, Solutions, and Recommendations

Topic Introduction

What enhancements or changes would you make to the Author's plan?

Reader's Topic Analysis

____

Reader's Conclusions and Recommendations

____

**Case Study 22: Primary Strategies to Build
the Climate Change Bridge**

Topic Introduction

Do you believe that no plan currently exists to solve climate change or transition from fossil fuels to alternative energies? Why or why not?

Reader's Topic Analysis

____

Reader's Conclusions and Recommendations

Case Study 23: Primary Strategies to Build the Climate Change Bridge

Topic Introduction

Discuss the author's three primary strategies to build the climate change bridge as outlined in chapter 13. Include your agreement or disagreement on their viability.

Reader's Topic Analysis

Reader's Conclusions and Recommendations

Case Study 24: Paying for the Climate Change Bridge

Topic Introduction

Do you agree with the author's plan to pay for the climate change bridge from chapter 21 of his second book? Why or why not?

Reader's Topic Analysis

Reader's Conclusions and Recommendations

Case Study 25: Paying for the Climate Change Bridge

Topic Introduction

Please list your recommendations for paying for the climate change bridge.

Reader's Topic Analysis

____

Reader's Conclusions and Recommendations

____

Case Study 26: Competitive Energy Technologies and Energy Diversification

Topic Introduction

Do you agree with the author's discussion of competitive energy technologies and energy diversification? Why or why not?

Reader's Topic Analysis

____

Reader's Conclusions and Recommendations

____

Case Study 27: The Great Water Opportunity from Global Warming

Topic Introduction

Do you agree with the author's discussion of the great water opportunity from global warming? Why or why not?

Reader's Topic Analysis

____

Reader's Conclusions and Recommendations

____

REFERENCES

1   Snejana Farberov, "Putin's State TV Propagandist Olga Skabeyeva Says 'World War III has already begun,'" *New York Post*, June 1, 2022, https://nypost.com/2022/06/01/putin-propagandist-olga-skabeyeva-says-world-war-iii-has-already-begun/.

2   Amit Chaturvedi, *NDTV*, April 16, 2022, https://www.ndtv.com/world-news/world-war-iii-has-begun-after-sinking-of-moskva-russian-state-tv-2890945.

3   Chloe Taylor, *CNBC*, March 7, 2022, https://www.cnbc.com/2022/03/07/russia-ukraine-bill-ackman-says-world-war-iii-likely-already-started.html.

4   DNA Web Team, *DNA*, April 19, 2022, https://www.dnaindia.com/analysis/report-dna-special-has-world-war-iii-already-begun-2947040.

5   The Week Staff, *The Week*, October 28, 2022, https://www.theweek.co.uk/92967/are-we-heading-towards-world-war-3.

6   Gerard O'Connell, *America*, June 14, 2022, https://www.americamagazine.org/politics-society/2022/06/14/pope-francis-war-ukraine-nato-243153.

7   AP, *CNBC*, July 19, 2022, https://www.cnbc.com/2022/07/20/china-threatens-strong-measures-if-pelosi-visits-taiwan.html.

8   *BBC*, June 11, 2022, https://www.bbc.com/news/world-asia-61768875.

9   *The Economist*, March 11, 2021, https://www.economist.com/asia/2021/03/11/americas-top-brass-responds-to-the-threat-of-china-in-the-pacific?utm_medium=cpc.adword.pd&utm_source=google&utm_campaign=a.22brand_pmax&utm_content=conversion.direct-response.anonymous&gclid=EAIaIQobChMIyIvCk7SH-QIVcgF9Ch10ogArEAMYASAAEgKAE_D_BwE&gclsrc=aw.ds.

10 Mark Heinrich, ed., *Reuters*, July 15, 2022, https://www.reuters.com/world/middle-east/irans-military-warns-us-against-threats-use-force-2022-07-15/.

11 Jana Winter, *Yahoo News*, July 13, 2022, https://news.yahoo.com/exclusive-u
s-government-warns-iran-may-try-to-kill-american-officials-in-revenge-for-ki
lling-top-general-162641423.html.

12 Associated Press, *CBC*, June 11, 2022, https://www.cbc.ca/news/world/
nicaragua-russia-troops-planes-1.6485691.

13 Guy Faulconbridge and Parisa Hafezi, *Reuters*, July 19, 2022, https://www.
reuters.com/world/putin-visits-iran-first-trip-outside-former-ussr-since
-ukraine-war-2022-07-18/.

14 FBI, accessed July 20, 2022, https://www.fbi.gov/investigate/
counterintelligence/the-china-threat.

15 Helen Davidson, *The Guardian*, January 1, 2022, https://www.
theguardian.com/world/2022/jan/20/china-warns-of-serious-consequences-
after-tracking-us-warship.

16 Mark Moore, *New York Post*, June 2, 2021, https://nypost.com/2021/06/02/
chinese-media-says-beijing-expanding-its-nuclear-arsenal/.

17 Keoni Everington, *Taiwan News*, February 22, 2022, https://www.taiwannews.
com.tw/en/news/4451661.

18 Dan De Luce and Ken Dilanian, *NBC News*, March 27, 2021, https://
www.nbcnews.com/politics/national-security/china-s-growing-firepower-
casts-doubt-whether-u-s-could-n1262148.

19 Zaini Majeed, *Republic World*, September 13, 2021, https://www.
republicworld.com/world-news/rest-of-the-world-news/day-will-come-soo
n-china-threatens-us-of-hawaii-incursion-for-entering-south-china-sea.html.

20 *ANI*, updated May 15, 2022, https://www.aninews.in/news/world/asia/china-warn
s-us-it-will-be-defeated-if-the-two-superpowers-go-to-war-report20210515194443/.

21 Kashish Tandon, *EurAsian Times*, July 20, 2021, https://eurasiantimes.com/
china-threatens-to-hunt-down-us-military-jets-if-they-again-land-in-taiwan/.

22 Alan Dupont, *The Diplomat*, July 8, 2020, https://thediplomat.com/2020/07/
the-us-china-cold-war-has-already-started/.

23 Bloomberg News, *Star Advertiser*, March 7, 2022, https://www.staradvertiser.
com/2022/03/07/breaking-news/china-warns-u-s-against-forming-pacific-
^kato-and-backing-taiwan/.

24 Bethany Dawson, "Putin Accused the US of Acting like God and Predicted
a New World Order in Bullish St Petersburg Speech," *Business Insider,*
June 18, 2022, https://www.businessinsider.com/putin-us-god-over-ukrain
e-crisis-new-world-order-coming-2022-6; Zheping Huang, "Chinese
President Xi Jinping Has Vowed to Lead the 'New World Order,'" *Quartz,*
February 22, 2017, https://qz.com/916382/chinese-president-xi-jinping-ha
s-vowed-to-lead-the-new-world-order/.

25 Paul Best, *Fox News*, August 10, 2022, https://www.foxnews.com/world/chin a-touts-relationship-russia-accuses-us-being-main-instigator-ukrainian-crisis.

26 Paul Best, *Fox News*, August 14, 2022, https://www.foxnews.com/world/puti n-tells-kim-jong-un-expand-constructive-bilateral-relations-north-korea-says.

27 AFP, *KYIV Post*, August 14, 2022, https://www.kyivpost.com/russias-war/ irans-top-automaker-sets-sights-on-russian-market-following-sanctions.html.

28 Elsa Maishman, *BBC News*, August 16, 2022, https://www.bbc.com/news/ world-europe-62550437.

29 Joel Gehrke, *Washington Examiner*, August 15, 2022, https://www. washingtonexaminer.com/policy/defense-national-security/russia-china- drone-ukraine-warfare.

30 Trevor Filseth, *National Interest*, August 16, 2022, https:// nationalinterest.org/blog/middle-east-watch/game-drones-iran-hosts-uav- competition-russia-and-belarus-204246.

31 Xander Landen, *Newsweek*, August 14, 2022, https://www.newsweek. com/putin-knows-he-made-mistake-ukraine-will-never-admit-it-stavridis- 1733490?amp=1#amp_tf=From%20%251%24s&aoh=16606682097702 &csi=0&referrer=https%3A%2F%2Fwww.google.com.

32 Luca Cacciatore, *Newsmax*, August 17, 2022, https://www.newsmax.com/ newsfront/china-russia-military-exercise/2022/08/17/id/1083550/.

33 Luke Tress, *Times of Israel*, August 17, 2022, https://www.timesofisrael. com/iran-linked-hacking-group-targeting-israeli-shipping-us-cybersecur ity-firm-says/.

34 Gabriela Bernal, *Nikkei Asia*, August 3, 2022, https://asia.nikkei.com/ Spotlight/N-Korea-at-crossroads/Russia-grows-closer-to-North-Korea- amid-international-isolation.

35 Jerusalem Post Staff, *Jerusalem Post*, August 19, 2022, https://www.jpost.com/ omg/article-715100.

36 Eyal Zisser, *Israel Hayom*, August 21, 2022, https://www.israelhayom.com/ opinions/iran-is-already-nuclearized-so-why-do-we-need-a-deal/.

37 Zoe Strozewski, *Newsweek*, August 10, 2022, https://www.newsweek.com/ putin-scrambling-support-outcasts-shows-his-weakness-expert-1732622.

38 Elizabeth Heckman, *Fox News*, July 27, 2022, https://www.foxnews.com/ media/idaho-sheriff-sends-dire-warning-idiotic-biden-officials-cusp- complete-collapse.

39 Landon Mion, *Fox News*, August 14, 2022, https://www.foxnews.com/ world/hundreds-mexican-national-guard-troops-sent-tijuana-over-car tel-fueled-violence.

40 Maria Yeryoma, *Kyiv Independent*, August 9, 2022. https://kyivindependent.com/regional/two-years-after-dictator-lukashenko-stole-the-election-belarus-is-a-grim-place.

41 Jay Clemons, Newsmax, August 16, 2022, https://www.newsmax.com/newsfront/russia-us-ukraine/2022/08/16/id/1083402/.

42 ZeroHedge, *Oil Price*, August 19, 2022, https://oilprice.com/Energy/Crude-Oil/Venezuela-Halts-Oil-Shipments-To-Europe-Demands-New-Concessions.html.

43 Oxford Business Group, *Oil Price*, August 21, 2022, https://oilprice.com/Geopolitics/International/Emerging-Markets-Rush-To-Join-BRICS-Alliance-As-High-Energy-Prices-Persist.html.

44 Charles Kennedy, *Oil Price*, August 5, 2022, https://oilprice.com/Energy/Crude-Oil/Russia-Displaces-Saudi-Arabian-Oil-In-India.html.

45 Phelim Kine, *Politico*, August 16, 2022, https://www.politico.com/news/2022/08/16/xi-jinping-saudi-arabia-trip-middle-east-influence-00052023.

46 Hudhaifa Ebrahim, *Jerusalem Post*, August 15, 2022, https://www.jpost.com/international/article-714744.

47 *CGTN*, July 19, 2022, https://news.cgtn.com/news/2022-07-19/China-India-hold-16th-corps-commander-level-meeting-on-border-issues-1bMQ7aTx3Fu/index.html.

48 *CGTN*, August 17, 2022, https://news.cgtn.com/news/2022-08-17/China-Uzbekistan-to-hold-6th-meeting-of-cooperation-committee-1czIhO79Q8o/index.html.

49 *CGTN*, July 9, 2022, https://news.cgtn.com/news/2022-07-09/Chinese-Canadian-FMs-vow-to-bring-bilateral-relations-back-on-track--1bwt5TipN04/index.html.

50 *CGTN*, August 17, 2022, https://news.cgtn.com/news/2022-08-17/China-Chile-vow-to-push-bilateral-relations-to-higher-level-1cznygRWlhe/index.html.

51 *CGTN*, August 12, 2022, https://news.cgtn.com/news/2022-08-12/China-is-world-s-2nd-largest-commercial-satellite-owner-1cqEZjfndny/index.html.

52 Seth D. Kaplan, *Wall Street Journal*, August 21, 2022, https://www.wsj.com/articles/how-chinas-propaganda-influences-the-west-state-media-cable-censorship-wechat-social-media-hong-kong-election-russia-ukraine-newspaper-11661108182?mod=mhp.

53 Reuters, *Fox News*, August 10, 2022, https://www.foxnews.com/world/uk-summons-chinese-ambassador-aggressive-escalation-taiwan.

54 Dzirhan Mahadzir, *USNI News*, August 16, 2022, https://news.usni.org/2022/08/16/u-s-joins-south-korea-australia-japan-canada-for-missile-defense-exercise-following-rimpac.

55 Brie Stimson, *Fox News*, August 18, 2022, https://www.foxnews.com/world/us-hold-wide-ranging-trade-talks-taiwan-tensions-china.

56 Jacob Fromer, *South China Morning Post*, August 18, 2022, https://www.scmp.com/news/china/military/article/3189277/next-north-korea-^kuclear-test-could-lead-us-deploy-strategic.

57 Katherine Fung, *Newsweek*, July 26, 2022, https://www.newsweek.com/russian-families-descend-kremlin-demand-truth-about-soldiers-1728116.

58 Patrick Howell O'Neill, *MIT Technology Review*, August 16, 2022. https://www.technologyreview.com/?p=1057894&preview=true&truid=&utm_source=the_download&utm_medium=email&utm_campaign=the_download.unpaid.engagement&utm_term=Active%20Qualified&utm_content=08-16-2022&mc_cid=4c2a4b06e2&mc_eid=7f625e5060.

59 June Teufel Dreyer, *Foreign Policy Research Institute*, June 6, 2022, https://www.fpri.org/article/2022/06/hong-kong-two-years-after-the-passage-of-the-national-security-act/.

60 Guy Taylor, *Washington Times*, July 20, 2022, https://www.washingtontimes.com/news/2022/jul/20/iranian-dissidents-reject-wests-appeasement-policy/.

61 Keith Zhai, August 19, 2022, https://www.wsj.com/articles/chinas-xi-considers-visiting-central-asia-potential-meeting-with-putin-next-month-11660916483?mod=mhp.

62 Irina Slav, August 1, 2022, https://oilprice.com/Energy/Crude-Oil/How-Russian-Oil-Is-Making-Its-Way-From-Europe-To-Asia.html.

63 Eric Mack, *Newsmax*, July 28, 2022, https://www.newsmax.com/newsfront/russia-defense-minister/2022/07/28/id/1080844/.

64 Andrew Stanton, *Newsweek*, July 30, 2022, https://www.newsweek.com/putin-regime-beginning-end-russia-expert-1729402?_gl=1.

65 Sandy Fitzgerald, Newsmax, August 12, 2022, https://www.newsmax.com/newsmax-tv/kellytshibaka-norad-russia/2022/08/12/id/1082883/.

66 AP, *Yahoo News*, August 5, 2022, https://news.yahoo.com/china-summons-european-diplomats-over-043739389.html.

67 Scott Neuman, August 5, 2022, https://www.npr.org/2022/08/05/1115731152/china-taiwan-military-drills-pelosi-visit.

68 Vanda Felbab-Brown, *Brookings*, February 4, 2022, https://www.brookings.edu/opinions/the-china-connection-in-mexicos-illegal-economies/.

69 U.S. Department of State, July 1, 2021, https://www.state.gov/forced-labor-in-chinas-xinjiang-region/.

70 Jay Clemons, *Newsmax*, August 17, 2022, https://www.newsmax.com/newsfront/united-nations-china-uyghurs/2022/08/17/id/1083560/.

71 Nichola Daunton, *Euronews.green*, updated August 4, 2022, https://www.euronews.com/green/2022/04/08/illegal-fishing-and-physical-violence-life-aboard-china-s-devil-vessels-revealed-in-new-re.

72   Nicole Sganga, *CBS News*, May 4, 2022, https://www.cbsnews.com/news/chinese-hackers-took-trillions-in-intellectual-property-from-about-30-multinational-companies/.

73   Michael Ellis, *Fox News*, July 29, 2022, https://www.foxnews.com/opinion/china-domestic-national-security-threat-biden.

74   Benjamin Weinthal, *Fox News*, August 7, 2022, https://www.foxnews.com/world/palestinian-islamic-jihads-rocket-barrages-israel-trace-irans-regional-tentacles-experts-say.

75   Dion Nissenbaum, *Wall Street Journal*, August 10, 2022, https://www.wsj.com/articles/iran-has-begun-training-russia-to-use-its-advanced-drones-u-s-says-11660135921.

76   Newsfront, *Newsmax*, August 14, 2022, https://www.newsmax.com/newsfront/elections-the-china-card/2022/08/14/id/1083028/.

77   John Bolton, *The Hill*, July 26, 2022, https://thehill.com/opinion/national-security/3572169-when-will-american-businesses-awaken-to-the-threat-of-chinese-espionage/.

78   William A. Galston, *Wall Street Journal*, March 9, 2021, https://www.wsj.com/articles/america-wakes-up-to-the-china-threat-11615311587.

79   Jessica Smith, *Yahoo Finance*, October 25, 2019, https://www.yahoo.com/video/gop-congressman-americans-lawmakers-are-waking-up-to-china-threat-135004552.html.

80   Gordon G. Chang, *Daily News*, November 14, 2021, https://www.nydailynews.com/opinion/ny-oped-awaken-to-the-china-threat-20211114-ppjokrcllza3vk7rw4edlk2bom-story.html.

81   Tim Brinkhof, July 25, 2022, https://bigthink.com/the-past/war-civilization-development/.

82   R. Jordan Prescott, "Goodbye Conventional War. It's Been Fun," *Modern War Institute at West Point*, March 21, 2019, https://mwi.usma.edu/goodbye-conventional-war-fun/.

83   John Grady, May 14, 2015, https://news.usni.org/2015/05/14/mattis-u-s-suffering-strategic-atrophy.

84   Andrew A. Michta, "China, Russia, and the West's Crisis of Disbelief," *Wall Street Journal*, August 7, 2022, https://www.wsj.com/articles/china-russia-and-the-wests-crisis-america-democracy-fight-military-threat-disarmament-cold-war-putin-xi-response-11659892566?mod=mhp; Walter Russell, "A Costly Passivity toward China," *Wall Street Journal*, August 8, 2022, https://www.wsj.com/articles/a-costly-passivity-toward-china-nancy-pelosi-taiwan-visit-military-buildup-diplomacy-pacific-japan-south-korea-investment-trade-security-11659991742?mod=mhp.

85 Zoe Strozewski, *Newsweek*, August 16, 2022, https://www.newsweek.com/russian-tv-host-vladimir-solovyov-promotes-nuclear-strike-nato-counter-military-superiority-1734135.

86 Ian Lovett, *Wall Street Journal*, August 19, 2022, https://www.wsj.com/articles/ukraines-southern-forces-wage-a-slow-campaign-to-wear-the-russians-down-11660906801?mod=mhp.

87 Sinead Baker, *Business Insider*, August 19, 2022, https://www.businessinsider.com/russia-intel-knew-but-didnt-tell-kremlin-ukraine-would-fight-ussia-report-2022-8.

88 John Psaropoulos, *Alijazeera*, August 18, 2022, https://www.aljazeera.com/news/2022/8/18/ukrainian-attacks-in-crimea-weaken-russias-military-capacity.

89 Brendan Cole, *Newsweek*, August 16, 2022, https://www.newsweek.com/black-sea-putin-crimea-snake-island-moskva-1734124.

90 Sophie Wingate, Independent, August 19, 2022, https://www.independent.co.uk/news/uk/vladimir-putin-crimea-ukraine-kremlin-jeremy-fleming-b2148556.html.

91 Will Vernon, *BBC News*, August 22, 2022, https://www.bbc.com/news/world-europe-62553629.

92 Dasl Yoon, *Wall Street Journal*, August 21, 2022, https://www.wsj.com/articles/u-s-south-korea-revive-live-military-drills-after-four-year-hiatus-11661074202.

93 Heather Mongilio, *USNI News*, August 8, 2022, https://news.usni.org/2022/08/08/u-s-will-continue-taiwan-strait-transits-fonops-in-western-pacific-despite-growing-tension-with-china.

94 Michael Lee, *Fox News*, August 11, 2022, https://www.foxnews.com/world/taiwan-rejects-chinas-one-country-two-systems-plan-island.

95 Gabriel Honrada, *Asia Times*, August 19, 2022, https://asiatimes.com/2022/08/guams-missile-defenses-to-get-a-massive-upgrade/.

96 Caitlin M. Kenney, *Defense One*, August 19, 2022, https://www.defenseone.com/threats/2022/08/the-army-brief-august-19-2022/376066/.

97 Alia Shoaib, *Business Insider*, August 21, 2022, https://www.businessinsider.com/taiwan-learns-ukraine-porcupine-strategy-defend-against-china-2022-8.

98 Brad Lendon, *CNN*, August 19, 2022, https://www.cnn.com/2022/08/19/china/china-taiwan-strait-new-normal-mic-intl-hnk-ml/index.html.

99 Mary Anastasia O'Grady, *Wall Street Journal*, July 17, 2022, https://www.wsj.com/articles/iran-and-a-suspicious-flight-to-argentina-airplane-crew-passports-investigation-jet-cyber-intelligence-venezuelan-agents-11658078058?mod=mhp.

100 Echo Xie, *South China Morning Post*, February, 13, 2022, https://www.scmp.com/news/china/diplomacy/article/3166763/china-building-nuclear-power-plant-argentina-it-looks-latin.

101 Tipp Insights Editorial Board, *Tipp Insights*, August 12, 2022, https://tippinsights.com/china-riding-the-pink-tide-in-south-america/.

102 Peter Aitken, *Fox News*, July 16, 2022, https://www.foxnews.com/world/chin
    a-seek-greater-role-haiti-un-security-council-extends-political-mission.

103 Benoit Faucon and Joe Parkinson, *Wall Street Journal*, August 21, 2022, https://
    www.wsj.com/articles/russia-wagner-group-mercenaries-mali-west-africa-
    11661099199?mod=mhp.

104 Victor I. Nava, *Washington Examiner*, August 9, 2022, https://www.
    washingtonexaminer.com/news/petraeus-afghanistan-incubator-islamist-
    extremism.

105 Jillian Smith, "National Security Concerns Arise as China Buys Up U.S.
    Farmland," *Komo News*, August 13, 2022, https://komonews.com/amp/
    news/nation-world/national-security-concerns-arise-as-china-buys-up-us-far
    mland-investors-chinese-espionage-nations-food-security-at-risk-united-sta
    tes-farms-usda-fufeng-group-usa; Michael Lee, "Russia Uses FBI Trump Raid
    to 'Foment Discord' and 'Amplify Tensions' in US, Expert Says," *Fox News*,
    August 14, 2022, https://www.foxnews.com/world/russia-uses-fbi-trump-rai
    d-foment-discord-amplify-tensions-us.

106 Sandra Erwin, August 9, 2022, https://spacenews.com/u-s-space-command-
    basing-decision-approaching-final-stretch/.

107 Everett Bledsoe, October 2, 2022, https://www.thesoldiersproject.org/ho
    w-many-us-military-bases-are-there-in-the-world/.

108 Andrew Chatzky and James McBride, "China's Massive Belt and Road
    Initiative," *Council on Foreign Relations*, January 1, 2020, https://www.cfr.
    org/backgrounder/chinas-massive-belt-and-road-initiative; Christopher
    Cairns, "China's Investment Setbacks in Panama," *The Diplomat*, February
    26, 2022, https://thediplomat.com/2022/02/chinas-investment-setbacks-in-
    panama/; Lauren Frayer, "Why a Chinese Ship's Arrival in Sri Lanka Has
    Caused Alarm in India and the West," *NPR*, August 19, 2022, https://www.
    npr.org/2022/08/19/1118113095/sri-lanka-china-ship-hambantota-port.

109 *Ukrinform*, "Another Russian Spy Busted in Ukraine," August 19, 2022,
    https://www.ukrinform.net/amp/rubric-ato/3553771-another-russian-spy-b
    usted-in-ukraine.html; Keith Zhai, "Southeast Asia Seeks to Tiptoe through
    U.S.-China Taiwan Minefield," *Wall Street Journal*, August 7, 2022, https://
    www.wsj.com/articles/southeast-asia-seeks-to-tiptoe-through-u-s-china-ta
    iwan-minefield-11659872556?mod=mhp; Ted Kemp and Lee Ying Shan, "U.S.
    Navy Is Seeing More 'Unsafe' Aerial Intercepts by China, Says Seventh Fleet
    Commander," *CNBC*, August 16, 2022, https://www.cnbc.com/2022/08/16/
    increase-in-unsafe-aerial-chinese-intercepts-us-navy.html.

110 Lawrence Richard, August 21, 2022, https://www.foxnews.com/
    world/daughter-top-putin-ally-alexander-dugin-pushed-ukraine-invas
    ion-killed-car-bomb-outside-moscow.

111 Nicolas Mazzucchi, June 8, 2022, https://www.nature.com/articles/d41586-022-01733-9.

112 Felicity Nelson, June 22, 2022, https://www.sciencealert.com/a-huge-step-forward-in-quantum-computing-was-just-announced-the-first-ever-quantum-circuit.

113 Gabriel Honrada, *Asia Times*, August 1, 2022, https://asiatimes.com/2022/08/china-south-korea-racing-for-stealth-fighter-supremacy/.

114 Colin Demarest, *Army Times*, July 27, 2022, https://www.armytimes.com/c2-comms/2022/07/27/us-army-sets-timeline-for-demo-of-new-hard-to-detect-mobile-command-post/.

115 Megan Eckstein, *Defense News*, August 1, 2022, https://www.defensenews.com/naval/2022/08/01/rimpac-lessons-will-inform-navys-pursuit-of-a-program-of-record-unmanned-ship-in-2025/.

116 Caitlin M. Kenney, *Defense One*, August 3, 2022, https://www.defenseone.com/technology/2022/08/robot-ships-debut-rimpac-helping-us-navy-sail-toward-less-crewed-future/375305/.

117 Amos Harel, *Haaretz*, August 5, 2022, https://www.haaretz.com/israel-news/security-aviation/2022-08-05/ty-article/.highlight/russia-ukraine-war-catapults-israeli-arms-industry-to-global-stage/00000182-69d0-d9e1-a1ae-f9f3637e0000.

118 Maksim Panasovskyi, *Gagadget.com*, April 8, 2022, https://gagadget.com/en/war/154089-northrop-grumman-received-329-billion-to-develop-a-missile-defense-system-that-could-protect-the-entire-us-territory-/.

119 ExxonMobil, *Wall Street Journal*, August 7, 2022, https://partners.wsj.com/exxonmobil/business-of-carbon-capture-and-storage/renewable-diesel-for-our-changing-world/?dclid=CJOmlsrktPkCFUtdwQod4g0AwA.

120 Yaro Trofimov, *Wall Street Journal*, August 7, 2022, https://www.wsj.com/articles/ukraines-drone-spotters-on-front-lines-wage-new-kind-of-war-11659870805.

121 Myroslav Trinko, *Gagadget.com*, August 6, 2022, https://gagadget.com/en/war/154802-atacms-replacement-lockheed-martin-is-developing-a-new-missile-for-himars-and-m270-with-a-range-of-up-to-650-km-it-wi/00.

122 Michael Lee, *Fox News*, August 8, 2022, https://www.foxnews.com/world/western-tech-continues-flow-russia-despite-sanctions-report.

123 Burak Ege Bekdil, *Yahoo News*, August 8, 2022, https://news.yahoo.com/turkey-defense-industry-eyes-export-092500414.html.

124 Victor I. Nava, *Washington Examiner*, August 9, 2022, https://www.washingtonexaminer.com/news/watch-russia-launches-iranian-satellite-into-space.

125 TOI Staff, *Times of Israel*, August 10, 2022, https://www.timesofisrael.com/new-iran-satellite-presents-significant-challenge-to-israel-us-and-allies-experts/.

126 AFP, *Times of Israel*, August 12, 2022, https://www.timesofisrael.com/iran-to-build-3-more-suspected-spy-satellites-as-concern-mounts-over-russia-ties/.

127 Ben Samuels and Avi Scharf, *Haaretz*, August 12, 2022, https://www.haaretz.com/israel-news/security-aviation/2022-08-12/ty-article/amid-drone-deal-irgc-linked-flights-to-russia-surge/00000182-8bcc-da98-abf6-bfdd2d710000.

128 Gabriel Honrada, *Asia Times*, August 8, 2022, https://asiatimes.com/2022/08/china-unveils-game-changing-electronic-warfare-drones/.

129 Megan Eckstein, *Yahoo News*, August 8, 2022, https://news.yahoo.com/us-navy-injects-first-kind-150000255.html.

130 Mark Gillispie, *AP News*, August 8, 2022, https://apnews.com/article/climate-and-environment-8dd0e4ad3345387ea72e83a506ef3a00.

131 Christopher McFadden, *Interesting Engineering*, August 9, 2022, https://interestingengineering.com/innovation/china-allegedly-developed-a-new-flying-submarine-drone-that-could-penetrate-aircraft-carrier-defenses.

132 Kim Tong-Hyung, *Defense News*, August 10, 2022, https://www.defensenews.com/global/asia-pacific/2022/08/10/china-south-korea-clash-over-thaad-anti-missile-system/.

133 Adam Button, *Forexlive*, August 9, 2022, https://www.forexlive.com/news/there-is-a-profound-disconnect-in-battery-metals-20220809/.

134 Ryan Dube, *Wall Street Journal*, August 10, 2022, https://www.wsj.com/articles/electric-cars-batteries-lithium-triangle-latin-america-11660141017?mod=mhp.

135 Didi Kirsten Tatlow, *Newsweek*, August 10, 2022, https://www.newsweek.com/2022/08/19/china-targets-israeli-technology-quest-global-dominance-us-frets-1727108.html.

136 Ben Knight, *Science X*, August 5, 2022, https://phys.org/news/2022-08-graphene-oxide-membranes-reveal-unusual.html.

137 Megan Eckstein, *Defense News*, August 10, 2022, https://www.defensenews.com/naval/2022/08/10/new-us-marine-regiment-shows-off-capabilities-at-rimpac-ahead-of-fall-experimentation-blitz/.

138 Ashish Danqwal, *Eurasian Times*, August 10, 2022, https://eurasiantimes.com/us-goes-the-hypersonic-way-to-develop-next-gen-artillery/?amp.

139 Andrew Eversden, *Breaking Defense*, August 10, 2022, https://breakingdefense.com/2022/08/bullet-made-out-of-light-army-to-send-first-stryker-mounted-combat-laser-to-soldiers-in-next-45-days/.

140 Sandra Erwin, *Space News*, August 10, 2022, https://spacenews.com/darpa-selects-companies-for-inter-satellite-laser-communications-project/.

141 Andrew Eversden, *Breaking Defense*, August 11, 2022, https://breakingdefense.com/2022/08/army-must-start-leaning-on-kinetic-options-for-counter-drone-as-autonomous-uas-proliferate/.

142 *Army Recognition*, August 12, 2022, https://www.armyrecognition.com/defense_news_august_2022_global_security_army_industry/lockheed_martins_next_generation_interceptor_hits_new_milestone.html.

143 Loukia Papadopoouloos, *Interesting Engineering*, August 13, 2022, https://interestingengineering.com/innovation/lockheed-martin-layered-laser-defense-system.

144 Jen Judson, Yahoo News, August 12, 2022, https://news.yahoo.com/missile-defense-agency-priorities-hypersonics-192404898.html.

145 Kyle Mizokami, *Yahoo News*, August 12, 2022, https://news.yahoo.com/ramjet-powered-artillery-u-ground-161000010.html.

146 Gabriel Honrada, *Asia Times*, August 12, 2022, https://asiatimes.com/2022/08/us-points-new-gen-missile-defense-radar-at-china-russia/.

147 Kris Osborn, *National Interest*, August 15, 2022, https://nationalinterest.org/blog/buzz/df-26-navy-has-plans-destroy-china%E2%80%99s-best-%E2%80%98carrier-killer%E2%80%99-missile-204202.

148 Thomas Novelly, *Yahoo News*, August 15, 2022, https://news.yahoo.com/space-force-takes-over-military-185337796.html.

149 Mariel Borowitz, *Yahoo News*, August 15, 2022, https://news.yahoo.com/war-ukraine-highlights-growing-strategic-123900157.html.

150 Maksim Panasovskyi, *Gagadget.com*, August 16, 2022, https://gagadget.com/en/war/157773-switzerland-will-abandon-the-american-m109-kawest-howitzer-in-favor-of-the-swedish-archer-or-german-rch-155-agm/.

151 Beatrice Nolan, *Business Insider*, August 15, 2022, https://www.businessinsider.com/baykar-drone-ukraine-manufacturing-factory-demand-bayraktar-tb2-drones-2022-8.

152 Sandra Erwin, *Space News*, August 15, 2022, https://spacenews.com/spacex-gets-1-9-million-air-force-contract-for-starlink-services-in-europe-and-africa/.

153 Constantine Atlamazoglou, *Business Insider*, August 15, 2022, https://www.businessinsider.com/poland-buys-south-korean-jets-to-replace-aging-soviet-fighters-2022-8.

154 Greg Hadley, *Air Force Magazine*, August 16, 2022, https://www.airforcemag.com/air-force-official-were-starting-to-lose-our-lead-on-propulsion/.

155 Christopher McFadden, *Interesting Engineering*, August 16, 2022, https://interestingengineering.com/innovation/us-military-tests-minuteman-intercontinental-missile.

156 Justin Katz, *Breaking Defense*, August 18, 2022, https://breakingdefense.com/2022/08/lockheed-delivers-high-energy-laser-four-years-in-the-making-to-us-navy/.

157 Sandra Erwin, *Space News,* August 17, 2022, https://spacenews.com/commercial-geospatial-technologies-that-detect-gps-disruptions-to-be-tested-in-military-exercises/.

158 John Grady, *USNI News*, August 18, 2022, https://news.usni.org/2022/08/18/chinas-navy-could-have-5-aircraft-carriers-10-ballistic-missile-subs-by-2030-says-csba-report.

159 Joe Saballa, *The Defense Post*, August 11. 2022, https://www.thedefensepost.com/2022/08/11/spain-themis-unmanned-vehicle/amp/#amp_tf=From%20%251%24s&aoh=16609246070711&csi=0&referrer=https%3A%2F%2Fwww.google.com.

160 Jen Judson, *Defense News*, August 18, 2022, https://www.defensenews.com/digital-show-dailies/smd/2022/08/18/the-us-army-digs-a-new-sandbox-for-its-laser-weapons/.

161 Maksim Panasovskyi, Gagadget.com, August 18, 2022, https://gagadget.com/en/weapons/158998-lockheed-martin-is-the-first-in-the-world-to-deliver-the-helios-laser-weapon-it-works-on-the-principle-of-the-dea/#!.

162 Tanmay Kadam, *EurAsian Times*, August 20, 2022, https://eurasiantimes.com/china-develops-anti-stealth-radar-so-small-that-it-could/.

163 Zeyi Yang, *MIT Technology Review*, August 18, 2022, https://www.technologyreview.com/2022/08/18/1058116/eda-software-us-china-chip-war/.

164 Colin Clark, *Breaking Defense*, August 19, 2022, https://breakingdefense.com/2022/08/upstart-anduril-australia-hopes-to-make-100s-of-large-drone-subs-itar-free-ceo-says/.

165 Sandra Erwin, *Space News*, August 18, 2022, https://spacenews.com/as-dod-shifts-to-smaller-satellites-new-questions-emerge-on-how-to-manage-rideshare-launches/.

166 Justin Katz, *Breaking Defense*, August 19, 2022, https://breakingdefense.com/2022/08/russias-naval-doctrine-may-call-for-challenging-the-west-but-does-it-have-the-shipyards/.

167 Maksim Panasovskyi, *Gagadget.com*, August 20, 2022, https://gagadget.com/en/weapons/159229-saudi-arabia-bought-the-best-american-thaad-air-defense-system-for-15-billion-and-will-prepare-four-sites-for-the/.

168 Molly Boigon and Courtney Kube, *NBC News*, June 27, 2022, https://www.nbcnews.com/news/military/every-branch-us-military-struggling-meet-2022-recruiting-goals-officia-rcna35078.

169 Steve Beynon, "Army Opens Its Doors to Recruits Who Fail to Meet Initial Body Fat and Academic Standards amid Recruiting Crisis," *Military.com*, July 26, 2022, https://www.military.com/daily-news/2022/07/26/army-opens-its-doors-recruits-who-fail-initial-body-fat-and-academic-tests-amid-recruiting-crisis.html; Chuck Devore, "Thanks to Leftist Corruption, U.S. Military Recruiting Is in Total Freefall," *The Federalist*, June 29, 2022, https://thefederalist.com/2022/06/29/thanks-to-leftist-corruption-u-s-military-recruiting-is-in-total-freefall/.

170 Mackenzie Eaglen, August 12, 2022, https://breakingdefense.com/2022/08/recruitment-is-now-a-real-threat-to-a-frail-force-facing-formidable-foes/.

171 Mackubin Ownes, "The Marines of the Future," Washington Examiner, April 7, 2022, https://www.washingtonexaminer.com/politics/the-marines-of-the-

future; Todd South, "Marines Eying the Overlooked Individual Ready Reserve to Keep Talent," *Marine Times*, April 17, 2022, https://www.marinecorpstimes.com/news/your-marine-corps/2022/04/17/marines-eying-the-overlooked-individual-ready-reserve-to-keep-talent/.

172 Francis P. Sempa, August 4, 2022, https://spectator.org/air-force-drag-queen-show-betrays-military-mission/.

173 Mark Barrott, "US Infrastructure Is Nowhere Near Ready for Biden's Electric Vehicle Timeline," *The Hill*, May 26, 2022, https://thehill.com/opinion/technology/3502897-us-infrastructure-is-nowhere-near-ready-for-bidens-electric-vehicle-timeline/; Tsvetana Paraskova, "Money Won't Solve America's Power Grid Problems," *Oil Price*, August 15, 2022, https://oilprice.com/Energy/Energy-General/Money-Wont-Solve-Americas-Power-r-Grid-Problems.html; Sandia National Laboratories, "Back to the Drawing Board: Reinventing Offshore Wind Turbines," *TechXplore*, August 16, 2022, https://techxplore.com/news/2022-08-board-reinventing-offshore-turbines.html.

174 Tim Schauenberg, "Water Scarcity: EU Countries Forced to Restrict Drinking Water Access," Deutsche Welle, July 7, 2022, https://www.dw.com/en/water-scarcity-eu-countries-forced-to-restrict-drinking-water-access/a-62363819; Julia Jacobo, "Sea Level Rise Is Expected to Worsen Coastal Flooding—Even on Sunny Days, According to New NOAA Report," *ABC News*, August 3, 2022. https://abcnews.go.com/US/sea-level-rise-expected-worsen-coastal-flooding-sunny/story?id=87874281; Alexander S. Kolker, "A New Storm Is Brewing in Struggle over Climate Change: Homeowner's Insurance," *The Hill*, August 2, 2022, https://thehill.com/opinion/energy-environment/3583414-a-new-storm-is-brewing-in-struggle-over-climate-change-homeowners-insurance/.

175 Phil Rosen, *Markets Insider*, August 8, 2022, https://markets.businessinsider.com/news/commodities/russian-oil-exports-italy-turkey-european-buyers-sanctions-war-ukraine-2022-8?amp=#amp_tf=From%20%251%24s&aoh=16600808152046&csi=0&referrer=https%3A%2F%2Fwww.google.com.

176 Roman Tsymbaliuk, *Ukrinform*, August 17, 2022, https://www.ukrinform.net/rubric-economy/3552107-russian-defense-industry-switching-to-247-operations.html.

177 Alex Kimani, *Oil Price*, August 2, 2022, https://oilprice.com/Energy/Energy-General/How-Commodity-Traders-Are-Helping-Fund-Russias-War.html.

178 Alex Kimani, *Oil Price*, August 8, 2022, https://oilprice.com/Energy/Energy-General/Offshore-Drilling-Is-Coming-Back-With-A-Bang.html.

179 Nexus Media, *Clean Technica*, August 11, 2022, https://cleantechnica.com/2022/08/10/top-coal-firm-in-world-cashing-in-on-global-energy-crisis/

amp/#amp_tf=From%20%251%24s&aoh=16602525225421&csi=0&referrer=https%3A%2F%2Fwww.google.com.

180 Phil Rosen, *Markets Insider*, August 11, 2022, https://markets.businessinsider.com/news/commodities/russian-oil-ship-to-ship-transfer-anonymous-chinese-buyer-sanctions-2022-8.

181 Post Editorial Board, *New York Post*, August 20, 2022, https://nypost.com/2022/08/20/germanys-painful-lesson-for-us-climate-warriors-on-the-dangers-of-going-green/.

182 Tsvetana Paraskova, *Oil Price*, August 21, 2022, https://oilprice.com/Energy/Crude-Oil/High-Impact-Oil-And-Gas-Drilling-Is-Back.html.

183 Carl Surran, "No New Refineries Likely Ever Built Again in the U.S., Chevron CEO Warns," *Seeking Alpha,* June 3, 2022, https://seekingalpha.com/news/3845705-no-new-refineries-likely-ever-built-again-in-the-us-chevron-ceo-warns; Tsvetana Paraskova, "Global Refining Capacity to Expand with New Projects in Middle East, Asia," *Oil Price*, August 2, 2022, https://oilprice.com/Latest-Energy-News/World-News/Global-Refining-Capacity-To-Expand-With-New-Projects-In-Middle-East-Asia.html; Brittany Cronin, "How a Massive Refinery Shortage Is Contributing to High Gas Prices," *NPR*, June 26, 2022, https://www.npr.org/2022/06/26/1107265390/refinery-shortage-high-gas-prices-russia.

184 Gavin Bade, *Politico*, February 19, 20222, https://www.politico.com/news/2022/02/19/china-investments-economy-us-congress-00008745.

185 Bethany G. Russell, *Military Review* 100, no. 5 (September-October 2020): 33–43, https://www.armyupress.army.mil/Journals/Military-Review/English-Edition-Archives/September-October-2020/Russell-Economic-Warfare/.

186 Michelle Chan, *Wall Street Journal*, July 29, 2022, https://www.wsj.com/articles/sec-adds-alibaba-to-list-of-chinese-companies-facing-delisting-11659130698.

187 Emma Loop, *Washington Examiner*, July 21, 2022, https://www.washingtonexaminer.com/news/western-companies-in-china-and-russia-eye-exits.

188 Su-Lin Tan, *CNBC*, June 28, 20222, https://www.cnbc.com/2022/06/28/new-g-7-infrastructure-plan-offers-alternative-to-china-belt-road-.html.

189 Ralph Jennings, *SCMP*, August 8, 2022, https://www.scmp.com/economy/global-economy/article/3188149/china-cuts-tariffs-cosies-16-worlds-poorest-nations-us?module=perpetual_scroll_0&pgtype=article&campaign=3188149.

190 Nik Martin, *DW*, August 17, 2022, https://www.dw.com/en/why-chinas-economy-is-in-trouble-and-what-it-means-for-you/a-62823625.

191 Elbridge A. Colby and Alexander B. Gray, *Wall Street Journal*, August 18, 2022, https://www.wsj.com/articles/americas-industrial-base-isnt-ready-for-war-with-china-weapons-defense-funding-military-war-conflict-taiwan-supplier-11660833718?mod=mhp.

192 Dion Rabouin, August 20, 2022, https://www.wsj.com/articles/
u-s-companies-on-pace-to-bring-home-record-number-of-overs
eas-jobs-11660968061?mod=mhp.

193 J. Peder Zane, *Real Clear Politics*, July 11, 2022, https://www.realclearpolitics.
com/articles/2022/07/11/the_physics_of_freedom_147865.html.

194 Fatma Khaled, "Putin Ally Lukashenko Faces Revolt from Officers against
Ukraine War: Report," *Newsweek*, July 10, 2022, https://www.newsweek.com/
putin-ally-lukashenko-faces-revolt-officers-against-ukraine-war-1723224;
Anthony B. Kim, "Why Economic Freedom Is More Integral to Foreign
Policy than Ever," *Washington Examiner*, May 5, 2022, https://www.
washingtonexaminer.com/restoring-america/courage-strength-optimism/wh
y-economic-freedom-is-more-integral-to-foreign-policy-than-ever.

195 Frank Wolf, *Fox News*, August 21, 2022, https://www.foxnews.com/opinion/
china-arrests-cardinal-zen-religious-freedom-faces-grim-future-hong-kong.

196 Rebecca Feng, August 11, 2022, https://www.wsj.com/articles/bursting-chines
e-housing-bubble-compounds-beijings-economic-woes-11660235003.

197 Jerry Dunleavy, *Washington Examiner*, July 31, 2022, https://www.
washingtonexaminer.com/policy/technology/tiktok-lobbyists-gop-and-
democrat-senators-congressmen-staffers.

198 Holman W. Jenkins, *Wall Street Journal*, July 29, 2022, https://www.wsj.
com/articles/why-pretend-green-pork-will-stop-climate-change-alternative-en
ergy-global-warming-lies-government-officials-11659129705?mod=mhp.

199 Gabriella Hoffman, *Real Clear Energy*, July 29, 2022, https://www.
realclearenergy.org/articles/2022/07/29/an_inconvenient_truth_esg_is_
fueling_inflation_woes_845052.html.

200 Jimmy Byrn, *Wall Street Journal*, July 29, 2022, https://www.wsj.com/articles/
what-if-they-gave-a-war-and-everybody-was-woke-military-recruitment-crt-t
raining-obesity-reading-labor-market-11659108526?mod=djemalertNEWS.

201 Jane Their, *Yahoo Finance*, August 1, 2022, https://finance.yahoo.com/news/
gen-zers-turn-tiktok-fantasies-182653160.html.

202 The Editorial Board, *Wall Street Journal*, August 2, 2022, https://www.wsj.
com/articles/joe-manchins-mountain-valley-pipeline-dream-democrats-
environmental-permitting-reforms-chuck-schumer-11659476809?mod=mhp.

203 Su-Lin Tan, *CNBC*, August 1, 2022, https://www.cnbc.com/2022/08/02/coa
l-consumption-is-expected-to-return-to-2013s-record-levels-iea.html.

204 Courtney Flatt and Laura Sullivan, *NPR*, August 3, 2022, https://www.npr.
org/2022/08/03/1114964240/new-battery-technology-china-vanadium.

205 Ross Kerber, *Reuters*, August 3, 2022, https://www.reuters.com/business/
sustainable-business/exclusive-missouri-attorney-general-investigates-mor
ningstar-over-esg-ratings-2022-08-03/.

206 Teny Sahakian, *Yahoo News*, August 4, 2022, https://news.yahoo.com/climat e-change-proposals-putting-american-060053559.html.

207 Chris Queen, *PJ Media*, August 6, 2022, https://pjmedia.com/columns/ chris-queen/2022/08/06/gaslighting-how-the-mainstream-media-tries-to-d rive-you-to-the-left-n1618882.

208 Joe Silverstein, *Fox News*, August 7, 2022, https://www.foxnews.com/media/la-time s-urges-biden-use-executive-powers-declare-national-climate-emergency.

209 Virginia Aabram, *Washington Examiner*, August 7, 2022, https://www. washingtonexaminer.com/news/senate/senate-passes-inflation-reduction-act- after-all-night-vote-series.

210 The Editorial Board, *Wall Street Journal*, August 8, 2022, https://www.wsj. com/articles/tilting-at-climate-windmills-chuck-schumer-joe-manchin-tax-c limate-bill-bjorn-lomborg-11659993292?mod=mhp.

211 Fox News Staff, Fox News, August 6, 2022, https://www.foxnews.com/ politics/democrats-inflation-reduction-act-economic-malpractice-economist.

212 Associated Press, *ABC News*, August 10, 2022, https://abcnews.go.com/ Business/wireStory/china-criticizes-us-chip-law-threat-trade-88189665.

213 Thomas Phippen, *Fox News*, August 11, 2022, https://www.foxnews. com/politics/tax-climate-bill-massively-expand-irs-union-almost-exclus ively-donates-democrats.

214 Charles Kennedy, August 12, 2022, https://oilprice.com/Energy/Crude-Oil/ Asia-Gobbles-Up-Cheap-US-Crude-At-OPECs-Expense.html.

215 Harry Robertson, August 17, 2022, https://markets.businessinsider.com/ news/commodities/china-imports-us-oil-rise-spurns-russian-crude-energy-i ndia-2022-8.

216 Post Editorial Board, *New York Post*, August 13, 2022, https://nypost. com/2022/08/13/bidens-created-our-bad-new-normal-and-hes-loving-it/.

217 Jeremy Beaman, *Washington Examiner*, August 14, 2022, https://www. washingtonexaminer.com/policy/energy-environment/green-groups-plan- ^kext-fight-inflation-reduction-act.

218 Karl Evers-Hillstrom, *The Hill*, August 13, 2022, https://thehill.com/ business-a-lobbying/3597520-shocked-and-disheartened-how-coal-count ry-is-reacting-to-manchins-climate-deal/.

219 Hannah Towey, *Yahoo News*, August 14, 2022, https://news.yahoo.com/ jpmorgan-ceo-jamie-dimon-why-145955451.html.

220 Allysia Finley, *Wall Street Journal*, August 14, 2022, https://www. wsj.com/articles/beijing-gets-a-great-leap-forward-from-congress- inflation-reduction-act-green-energy-subsidies-innovation-price-contr ols-capitalism-xi-jinping-11660502287?mod=mhp.

221 Haisten Willis, *Washington Examiner*, August 18, 2022, https://www.washingtonexaminer.com/news/white-house/define-inflation-reduction-act.

222 Charles Creitz, *Fox News*, August 21, 2022, https://www.foxnews.com/media/biden-officials-push-electric-cars-recession-wary-americans-policy-fantasyland-expert.

223 Shel Evergreen, May 2, 2022, https://arstechnica.com/science/2022/05/elephant-in-the-room-clean-energys-need-for-unsustainable-minerals/.

224 Richard Backhaus, "Battery Raw Materials – Where from and Where To?" *National Library of Medicine* 123, no. 9 (August 27, 2021): 8–13, https://www.ncbi.nlm.nih.gov/pmc/articles/PMC8390110/.

225 Camila Domonoske, NPR, February 21, 2022, https://www.npr.org/2022/02/21/1082172649/how-china-dominates-the-electric-vehicle-supply-chain#:~:text=DOMONOSKE%3A%20In%20fact%2C%20when%20it,on%20China%20for%20these%20minerals.

226 Simon Wilson, *Money Week*, January 8, 2022, https://moneyweek.com/investments/commodities/industrial-metals/604306/china-cobalt-electric-car-batteries.

227 Lili Pike, *GRID*, January 18, 2022, https://www.grid.news/story/global/2022/01/18/china-is-owning-the-global-battery-race-that-could-be-a-problem-for-the-us/.

228 Trefor Moss, *Wall Street Journal*, November 3, 2019, https://www.wsj.com/articles/how-china-positioned-itself-to-dominate-the-future-of-electric-cars-11572804489.

229 John Xie, *VOA*, September 1, 2020, https://www.voanews.com/a/silicon-valley-technology_how-china-dominates-global-battery-supply-chain/6195257.html.

230 Ashutosh Pandey, *Deutsche Welle*, March 14, 2022, https://www.dw.com/en/chinese-graphite-dominance-threatens-electric-car-ambitions/a-60888876.

231 Sayumi Take, *NIKKEI Asia*, July 7, 2022, https://asia.nikkei.com/Business/Energy/China-s-solar-panel-supply-chain-domination-cause-for-worry-IEA#:~:text=China%20now%20holds%20a%20market,of%20global%20demand%2C%20it%20said.

232 Felicity Bradstock, *Oil Price*, August 21, 2022, https://oilprice.com/Energy/Energy-General/China-Accounts-For-Nearly-Half-Of-The-Worlds-Renewable-Energy-Capacity.html.

233 Caitlan McFall, *Fox Business*, July 28, 2022, https://www.foxbusiness.com/economy/world-economic-forum-calls-reduce-private-vehicles-by-eliminating-ownership.

234 Brian Gicheru Kinyua, *Maritime Executive*, July 29, 2022, https://maritime-executive.com/article/drought-threatens-major-rivers-in-the-u-s-and-europe.

235 Andrei Chirileasa, *Romania-Insider*, July 25, 2022, https://www.romania-insider.com/danube-flow-romania-low-july-2022.

236 *Watchers*, August 5, 2022, https://watchers.news/2022/08/05/rhine-river-drops-to-record-lows-restricting-shipping-and-exacerbating-the-european-energy-crisis/.

237 Aspen Pflughoeft, *Miami Herald*, August 12, 2022, https://www.miamiherald.com/news/nation-world/world/article264446131.html.

238 Joshua Askew, *Euro News*, August 14, 2022, https://www.euronews.com/2022/08/13/the-water-wasnt-there-shrinking-of-italys-lake-garda-shocks-tourists.

239 Elaina Hancock, *Science X*, August 5, 2022, https://phys.org/news/2022-08-advance-drought.html.

240 Dale Gavlak, *VOA*, June 20, 2022, https://www.voanews.com/a/un-experts-warn-of-serious-water-problems-for-iraq-/6625446.html.

241 *Alarabiya News*, July 16, 2022, https://english.alarabiya.net/News/middle-east/2022/07/16/Facing-drought-Iraq-asks-Turkey-to-release-more-water-along-Tigris-Euphrates-rivers.

242 Faris al-Omran, *AL-MASHAREQ*, June 1, 2022, https://almashareq.com/en_GB/articles/cnmi_am/features/2022/06/01/feature-01.

243 Mohamed Sabry, *AL-Monitor*, June 28, 2022, https://www.al-monitor.com/originals/2022/06/egypt-build-desalination-plant-iraq.

244 Natalie Croker, Renée Rigdon, Judson Jones, Carlotta Dotto, and Angela Dewan, *CNN*, August 20, 2022, https://www.cnn.com/2022/08/20/world/rivers-lakes-drying-up-drought-climate-cmd-intl/index.html.

245 *Newsmax*, August 21, 2022, https://www.newsmax.com/world/globaltalk/china-drought/2022/08/21/id/1083944/.

246 Jim Carlton, Matthew Dalton, and Sha Hua, *Wall Street Journal*, August 21, 2022, https://www.wsj.com/articles/droughts-hurt-worlds-largest-economies-11661087554?mod=mhp.

247 Reuters, *Yahoo News*, August 20, 2022, https://news.yahoo.com/plunging-water-levels-chinas-yangtze-182353400.html.

248 The Berkey, accessed August 14, 2022, https://theberkey.com/blogs/water-filter/marine-debris-and-ocean-pollution-in-hawaii#:~:text=Hawaii%20now%20includes%20warning%20signs,the%20Hawaiian%20beaches%20each%20year.

249 Murray Hiebert, *The Diplomat*, January 14, 2022, https://thediplomat.com/2022/01/the-looming-environmental-catastrophe-in-the-south-china-sea/.

250 Pratnashree Basu and Aadya Chaturvedi, *Observer Research Foundation*, March 8, 2021, https://www.orfonline.org/research/in-deep-water-current-threats-to-the-marine-ecology-of-the-south-china-sea/.

251 Ryan McNamara, *New Security Beat*, November 13, 2020, https://www.newsecuritybeat.org/2020/10/environmental-collateral-damage-south-china-sea-conflict/.

252 Katie Brigham, *CNBC*, August 3, 2022, https://www.cnbc.com/2022/08/03/how-to-clean-the-worlds-most-polluted-rivers.html.

253 Robert Lee Hotz, *Wall Street Journal*, February 12, 2015, https://www.wsj.com/articles/which-countries-create-the-most-ocean-trash-1423767676.

254 David Stanway and Muyu Xu, *Reuters*, October 29, 2019, https://www.reuters.com/article/us-china-pollution-oceans/chinas-ocean-waste-surges-27-in-2018-ministry-idUSKBN1X80FL.

255 Hannah Leung, *Forbes*, August 10, 2022, https://www.forbes.com/sites/hannahleung/2018/04/21/five-asian-countries-dump-more-plastic-than-anyone-else-combined-how-you-can-help/?sh=7c210d441234.

256 Echo Huang, *Quartz*, June 14, 2017, https://qz.com/1004589/80-of-plastic-in-the-ocean-can-be-traced-back-to-asias-rivers-led-by-china-indonesia-myanmar-a-study-by-netherland-based-the-ocean-cleanup-found/.

257 Nabiha Shahab, *China Dialogue Ocean*, June 9, 2021, https://chinadialogueocean.net/en/pollution/17615-indonesias-plastic-waste-emergency/.

258 Andrea Miller, *CNBC*, June 5, 2022, https://www.cnbc.com/2022/06/05/why-the-global-soil-shortage-threatens-food-medicine-and-the-climate.html.

259 Associated Press, *NPR*, August 11, 2022, https://www.npr.org/2022/08/11/1116874946/scientists-say-landfills-release-more-planet-warming-methane-than-previously-tho.

260 Dan Novak, August 14, 2022, https://learningenglish.voanews.com/a/satellites-show-landfills-releasing-large-amount-of-methane/6697742.html.

261 *Green Science Policy Institute*, August 2, 2022, https://phys.org/news/2022-08-pfas-antarctica-tibetan-plateau-rainwater.html.

262 Carly Cassella, *Science Alert*, August 5, 2022, https://www.sciencealert.com/its-raining-forever-chemicals-and-some-researchers-argue-there-s-no-going-back.

263 Sharon Udasin, *The Hill*, August 8, 2022, https://thehill.com/policy/equilibrium-sustainability/3593017-scientists-link-forever-chemical-exposure-to-development-of-liver-cancer/.

264 Andy Miller, *Atlanta Journal-Constitution*, August 8, 2022, https://www.ajc.com/life/health/epa-action-boosts-grassroots-momentum-to-reduce-toxic-forever-chemicals/JJHMK7ZN65AELG55CHPQFRBKH4/.

265 Yujie Xue, *South China Morning Post*, August 7, 2022, https://www.scmp.com/business/article/3187849/chinese-green-ambitions-dirty-side-beijing-faces-recycling-challenge?module=perpetual_scroll_0&pgtype=article&campaign=3187849.

266 *Stop These Things*, February 4, 2022, https://stopthesethings.com/2022/02/04/not-green-offshore-wind-industry-destroying-fishing-grounds-birds-marine-life/.

267 Ronn Blitzer, *Fox News*, August 14, 2022, https://www.foxnews.com/politics/nearly-one-year-afghanistan-exit-gen-keane-says-were-right-back-where-we-started.

268 Mstyslav Chernov, *The Diplomat*, December 10, 2021, https://thediplomat. com/2021/12/afghanistan-shrivels-in-worst-drought-in-decades/.

269 Assem Mayar, *Afghanistan Analysts Network*, November 6, 2021. https:// www.afghanistan-analysts.org/en/reports/economy-development-environment/global-warming-and-afghanistan-drought-hunger-and-thirst-e xpected-to-worsen/.

270 Fazelminallah Qazizai, *New Lines*, June 15, 2022, https://newlinesmag.com/ newsletter/in-afghanistan-a-drought-highlights-the-climate-crisis/.

271 Asia Pacific Office, *IFRC*, June 17, 2022, https://www.ifrc.org/press-release/ afghanistan-hunger-and-poverty-surge-drought-persists.

272 Umair Irfan, *VOX*, August 16, 2022, https://www.vox.com/23292669/drough t-2022-power-energy-grid-lake-mead-climate-heat-hoover-dam.

273 Will Daniel, *Fortune*, August 20, 2022, https://fortune.com/2022/08/20/chin a-heatwave-supply-chain-covid-lockdowns/.

274 Matt Bowen, "Why the United States Should Remain Engaged on Nuclear Power: Geopolitical and National Security Considerations," *Columbia SIPA Center on Global Energy Policy*, September 2020, https://www.energypolicy. columbia.edu/sites/default/files/file-uploads/Nuclear_Geopolitics_CGEP_ Commentary_FINAL.pdf (emphasis mine).

275 Catherine Clifford, *CNBC*, July 1, 2021, https://www.cnbc.com/2022/07/01/ russian-and-chinese-designs-in-87percent-of-new-nuclear-reactors-iea-chief. html#:~:text=Russian%20and%20Chinese%20designs%20dominate%20 nuclear%20reactors%2C%20warns%20IEA%20chief,-Published%20 Fri%2C%20Jul&text=Since%202017%2C%2087%25%20of%20 the,market%20leadership%2C%E2%80%9D%20Birol%20said.

276 Timothy Gardner, *Reuters*, July 27, 2022, https://www.reuters.com/business/ energy/us-selects-test-plant-advanced-nuclear-reactor-fuel-2022-07-27/.

277 Huileng Tan, *Business Insider*, July 28, 2022, https://www.businessinsider. com/germany-delay-nuclear-energy-plant-exit-russia-natural-gas-cut-2022-7.

278 Joel Gehrke, *Washington Examiner*, August 1, 2022, https://www.washingtonexaminer. com/policy/defense-national-security/japan-fears-putin-nuclear-bombs.

279 WIRED, *Ars Technica*, July 22, 2022, https://arstechnica.com/science/2022/07/ nuclear-power-plants-are-struggling-to-stay-cool/?amp=1.

280 TOI Staff, *Times of Israel*, August 3, 2022, https://www.timesofisrael.com/ira n-nuclear-program-moving-ahead-very-fast-warns-iaea-head/.

281 Edith M. Lederer, *AP News*, August 3, 2022, https://apnews.com/article/ russia-ukraine-science-accidents-d2e0077af104f2692b76f737c58e1984.

282 Lars Paulsson, *Bloomberg*, August 3, 2022, https://www.bloomberg.com/news/ articles/2022-08-03/edf-to-curb-nuclear-output-as-french-energy-crisis-worsens.

283 Julianne Geiger, *Oil Price*, August 3, 2022, https://oilprice.com/Latest-Energy-News/World-News/German-Chancellor-Germany-Could-Keep-Nuclear-Power-Plants-Operating-After-All.html.

284 Catherine Clifford, *CNBC*, August 3, 2022, https://www.cnbc.com/2022/08/03/nuclear-energy-growing-popularity-could-be-undone-by-one-accident.html.

285 Caroline Delbert, *Yahoo Finance*, August 3, 2022, https://finance.yahoo.com/news/tiny-modular-nuclear-reactor-just-184500363.html.

286 *Reuters*, August 4, 2022, https://www.reuters.com/business/energy/energy-crisis-revives-nuclear-power-plans-globally-2022-08-04/.

287 Anmar Frangoul, CNBC, August 5, 2022, https://www.cnbc.com/2022/08/05/goldman-doesnt-see-nuclear-as-a-transformational-tech-for-the-future.html.

288 Tom Pegden, *Business Live*, August 4, 2022, https://www.business-live.co.uk/manufacturing/rolls-royce-working-300m-department-24662057.

289 Keegan Hamilton, *Vice News*, August 4, 2022, https://www.vice.com/en/article/epzz87/california-nuclear-power-climate-change.

290 George Wright, *BBC News*, August 6, 2022, https://www.bbc.com/news/world-europe-62449982.

291 Brady Knox, *Washington Examiner*, August 8, 2022, https://www.washingtonexaminer.com/policy/foreign/russia-announces-temporary-withdrawal-new-start-treaty.

292 Dylan Carter, *Brussels Times*, August 8, 2022, https://www.brusselstimes.com/268817/russian-forces-threaten-to-blow-up-europes-largest-nuclear-reactor.

293 Lizzie Philip, *The Verge*, August 9, 2022, https://www.theverge.com/2022/8/9/23283165/russia-ukraine-war-us-uranium.

294 Brian Wang, *Next Big Future*, August 7, 2022, https://www.nextbigfuture.com/2022/08/france-will-spend-10-billion-euros-to-relaunch-nuclear-energy.html.

295 Brian Wang, *Next Big Future*, August 7, 2022, https://www.nextbigfuture.com/2022/08/california-and-germany-could-save-nuclear-reactors.html#amp_tf=From%20%251%24s&aoh=16600808152046&csi=0&referrer=https%3A%2F%2Fwww.google.com.

296 Angeli Gabriel, *Fox Weather*, August 1, 2022, https://www.foxweather.com/earth-space/florida-crocodiles-nuclear-plant-turkey-point?cmpid=hp1r_foxweather_obtest&dicbo=v1-7f5198ed1b5fe2843114fa1af7c580c2-00e17b74303517cbe6bf08cea931e9f870-gmzwczjrgiytcllfgvsgcljumzsgmljyg42dellggfqwcnjqgbstey3fmy.

297 Dow, August 9, 2022, https://corporate.dow.com/en-us/news/press-releases/dow--x-energy-to-drive-carbon-emissions-reductions-through-deplo.

298 Brendan Cole, *Newsweek*, August 9, 2022, https://www.newsweek.com/russi
a-ukraine-missiles-nuclear-warning-zaporizhzhya-britain-us-1732059.

299 Beatrice Nolan, *Business Insider*, August 9, 2022, https://www.
businessinsider.com/energy-french-power-stations-environmental-rules-heatw
ave-europe-2022-8.

300 Tara Copp, *Defense One*, August 11, 2022, https://www.defenseone.com/
threats/2022/08/us-military-furiously-rewriting-nuclear-deterrence-address-r
ussia-and-china-stratcom-chief-says/375725/.

301 Teri Schultz, *Deutsche Welle*, November 8, 2022, https://www.dw.com/en/
finns-say-yes-to-nuclear-waste/a-62779844.

302 Joel Gehrke, *Washington Examiner*, August 12, 2022, https://www.
washingtonexaminer.com/policy/defense-national-security/russia-threatens-
sabotage-european-nuclear.

303 NEI, accessed August 13, 2022, https://www.nei.org/fundamentals/
advanced-nuclear.

304 Daniel G. Jennings, *Medium*, August 3, 2022, https://marketmadhouse.medium.
com/us-small-modular-reactor-production-can-begin-b01a0547545c.

305 Tsvetana Paraskova, *Oil Price*, August 15, 2022, https://oilprice.com/
Latest-Energy-News/World-News/Bill-Gates-Backed-Firm-Raise
s-750M-To-Develop-Small-Nuclear-Reactors.html.

306 Howard Lee, *Ars Technica*, August 17, 2022, https://arstechnica.com/
science/2022/08/solving-the-rock-hard-problem-of-nuclear-waste-disposal/.

307 "5 Facts about Spent Nuclear Fuel," Office of Nuclear Energy, March 30, 2020,
https://www.energy.gov/ne/articles/5-fast-facts-about-spent-nuclear-fuel.

308 Kelsey Adkisson, "Recycling Gives New Purpose to Spent Nuclear Fuel,"
Pacific Northwest National Laboratory, May 14, 2021, https://www.pnnl.
gov/news-media/recycling-gives-new-purpose-spent-nuclear-fuel; Catherine
Clifford, "The Energy in Nuclear Waste Could Power the U.S. for 100
Years, but the Technology Was Never Commercialized," *CNBC*, June 2,
2022, https://www.cnbc.com/2022/06/02/nuclear-waste-us-could-power-th
e-us-for-100-years.html; *World Nuclear Association*. "What Is Nuclear Waste,
and What Do We Do with It?" accessed August 17, 2022, https://world-nuclear.
org/nuclear-essentials/what-is-nuclear-waste-and-what-do-we-do-with-it.aspx.

BIBLIOGRAPHY

Aabram, Virginia. "Senate Passes Inflation Reduction Act after All-Night Vote Series." *Washington Examiner*, August 7, 2022. https://www.washingtonexaminer.com/news/senate/senate-passes-inflation-reduction-act-after-all-night-vote-series.

Adkisson, Kelsey. "Recycling Gives New Purpose to Spent Nuclear Fuel." *Pacific Northwest National Laboratory*, May 14, 2021. https://www.pnnl.gov/news-media/recycling-gives-new-purpose-spent-nuclear-fuel.

AFP. "Iran to Build 3 More Suspected Spy Satellites as Concern Mounts over Russia Ties." *Times of Israel*, August 12, 2022. https://www.timesofisrael.com/iran-to-build-3-more-suspected-spy-satellites-as-concern-mounts-over-russia-ties/.

AFP. "Iran's Top Automaker Sets Sights on Russian Market Following Sanctions." *KYIV Post*, August 14, 2022. https://www.kyivpost.com/russias-war/irans-top-automaker-sets-sights-on-russian-market-following-sanctions.html.

Aitken, Peter. "China May Seek Greater Role in Haiti as UN Security Council Extends Political Mission." *Fox News*, July 16, 2022. https://www.foxnews.com/world/china-seek-greater-role-haiti-un-security-council-extends-political-mission.

Alarabiya News, "Facing Drought, Iraq Asks Turkey to Release More Water along Tigris, Euphrates Rivers." July 16, 2022. https://english.

alarabiya.net/News/middle-east/2022/07/16/Facing-drought-Iraq-asks-Turkey-to-release-more-water-along-Tigris-Euphrates-rivers.

Al-Omran, Faris. "Conflicts Exacerbate Drought That Threatens Millions in Syria, Iraq." AL-MASHAREQ, June 1, 2022. https://almashareq.com/en_GB/articles/cnmi_am/features/2022/06/01/feature-01.

ANI. "China Warns US It Will Be Defeated if the Two Superpowers Go to War." Updated May 15, 2022. https://www.aninews.in/news/world/asia/china-warns-us-it-will-be-defeated-if-the-two-superpowers-go-to-war-report20210515194443/.

AP. "China Halts Climate, Military Ties over Pelosi Taiwan Visit." *Yahoo News,* August 5, 2022. https://news.yahoo.com/china-summons-european-diplomats-over-043739389.html.

AP. "China Threatens 'Strong Measures' if Pelosi Visits Taiwan." *CNBC,* July 19, 2022. https://www.cnbc.com/2022/07/20/china-threatens-strong-measures-if-pelosi-visits-taiwan.html.

Army Recognition. "Lockheed Martin's Next Generation Interceptor Hits New Milestone." August 12, 2022. https://www.armyrecognition.com/defense_news_august_2022_global_security_army_industry/lockheed_martins_next_generation_interceptor_hits_new_milestone.html.

Asia Pacific Office, "Afghanistan: Hunger and Poverty Surge as Drought Persists." *IFRC,* June 17, 2022. https://www.ifrc.org/press-release/afghanistan-hunger-and-poverty-surge-drought-persists.

Askew, Joshua. "'The Water Wasn't There': Shrinking of Italy's Lake Garda Shocks Tourists." *Euro News,* August 14, 2022. https://www.euronews.com/2022/08/13/the-water-wasnt-there-shrinking-of-italys-lake-garda-shocks-tourists.

Associated Press. "China Criticizes US Chip Law as Threat to Trade." *ABC News,* August 10, 2022. https://abcnews.go.com/Business/wireStory/china-criticizes-us-chip-law-threat-trade-88189665.

Associated Press. "Nicaragua Authorizes Entry of Russian Troops, Planes, Ships." *CBC,* June 11, 2022. https://www.cbc.ca/news/world/nicaragua-russia-troops-planes-1.6485691.

Associated Press. "Scientists Say Landfills Release More Planet-Warming Methane than Previously Thought." *NPR*, August 11, 2022. https://www.npr.org/2022/08/11/1116874946/scientists-say-landfills-release-more-planet-warming-methane-than-previously-tho.

Atlamazoglou, Constantine. "NATO Member Poland Is Going to Asian Powerhouse to Find a Replacement for Its Aging Soviet-Era Fighter Jets." *Business Insider*, August 15, 2022. https://www.businessinsider.com/poland-buys-south-korean-jets-to-replace-aging-soviet-fighters-2022-8.

Backhaus, Richard. "Battery Raw Materials—Where from and Where To?" *National Library of Medicine* 123, no. 9 (August 27, 2021): 8–13. https://www.ncbi.nlm.nih.gov/pmc/articles/PMC8390110/.

Bade, Gavin. "'We're in an Economic War:' White House, Congress Weigh New Oversight of U.S. Investments in China." *Politico*, February 19, 20222. https://www.politico.com/news/2022/02/19/china-investments-economy-us-congress-00008745.

Baker, Sinead. "Russian Intelligence Knew That Ukrainians Would Not Welcome Russia, But Still Told the Kremlin They Would, Report Says." *Business Insider*, August 19, 2022. https://www.businessinsider.com/russia-intel-knew-but-didnt-tell-kremlin-ukraine-would-fight-ussia-report-2022-8.

Barrott, Mark. "US Infrastructure Is Nowhere Near Ready for Biden's Electric Vehicle Timeline." *The Hill*, May 26, 2022. https://thehill.com/opinion/technology/3502897-us-infrastructure-is-nowhere-near-ready-for-bidens-electric-vehicle-timeline/.

Basu, Pratnashree, and Aadya Chaturvedi. "In Deep Water: Current Threats to the Marine Ecology of the South China Sea." *Observer Research Foundation*, March 8, 2021. https://www.orfonline.org/research/in-deep-water-current-threats-to-the-marine-ecology-of-the-south-china-sea/.

BBC. "China Warns Taiwan Independence Would Trigger War." June 11, 2022. https://www.bbc.com/news/world-asia-61768875.

Beaman, Jeremy. "Green Groups Gear up for Next Climate Fight as Historic Bill Clears Congress." *Washington Examiner*, August 14, 2022.

https://www.washingtonexaminer.com/policy/energy-environment/green-groups-plan-next-fight-inflation-reduction-act.

Bekdil, Burak Ege. "Turkey's Defense Industry Eyes Export Expansion as Government Navigates Geopolitical Stage." *Yahoo News*, August 8, 2022. https://news.yahoo.com/turkey-defense-industry-eyes-export-092500414.html.

Berkey, The. "Marine Debris and Ocean Pollution in Hawaii—Plastics Are Becoming a Big Problem." Accessed August 14, 2022. https://theberkey.com/blogs/water-filter/marine-debris-and-ocean-pollution-in-hawaii#:~:text=Hawaii%20now%20includes%20warning%20signs,the%20Hawaiian%20beaches%20each%20year.

Bernal, Gabriela. "Russia Grows Closer to North Korea amid International Isolation." *Nikkei Asia*, August 3, 2022. https://asia.nikkei.com/Spotlight/N-Korea-at-crossroads/Russia-grows-closer-to-North-Korea-amid-international-isolation.

Best, Paul. "China Touts Relationship with Russia, Accuses US of Being 'Main Instigator of the Ukrainian Crisis.'" *Fox News*, August 10, 2022. https://www.foxnews.com/world/china-touts-relationship-russia-accuses-us-being-main-instigator-ukrainian-crisis.

Best, Paul. "Putin Tells Kim Jong-Un That They Will Expand 'Constructive Bilateral Relations,' North Korea Says." *Fox News*, August 14, 2022. https://www.foxnews.com/world/putin-tells-kim-jong-un-expand-constructive-bilateral-relations-north-korea-says.

Beynon, Steve. "Army Opens Its Doors to Recruits Who Fail to Meet Initial Body Fat and Academic Standards amid Recruiting Crisis." *Military.com*, July 26, 2022. https://www.military.com/daily-news/2022/07/26/army-opens-its-doors-recruits-who-fail-initial-body-fat-and-academic-tests-amid-recruiting-crisis.html.

Bledsoe, Everett. "How Many US Military Bases Are There in the World?" *Soldiers Project*, October 2, 2022. https://www.thesoldiersproject.org/how-many-us-military-bases-are-there-in-the-world/.

Blitzer, Ronn. "Nearly 1 Year after Afghanistan Exit, Gen. Keane Says 'We're Right Back Where We Started' in 2001." *Fox News*,

August 14, 2022. https://www.foxnews.com/politics/nearly-one-yea r-afghanistan-exit-gen-keane-says-were-right-back-where-we-started.

Bloomberg News. "China Warns U.S. against Forming Pacific NATO and Backing Taiwan." *Star Advertiser,* March 7, 2022. https:// www.staradvertiser.com/2022/03/07/breaking-news/china-warns- u-s-against-forming-pacific-nato-and-backing-taiwan/.

Boigon, Molly, and Courtney Kube. "Every Branch of the Military Is Struggling to Make Its 2022 Recruiting Goals, Officials Say." *NBC News,* June 27, 2022. https://www.nbcnews.com/ news/military/every-branch-us-military-struggling-meet-2022- recruiting-goals-officia-rcna35078.

Bolton, John. "When Will American Businesses Wake Up to the Threat of Chinese Espionage?" *The Hill*, July 26, 2022. https://thehill.com/ opinion/national-security/3572169-when-will-american-businesse s-awaken-to-the-threat-of-chinese-espionage/.

Borowitz, Mariel. "War in Ukraine Highlights the Growing Strategic Importance of Private Satellite Companies—Especially in Times of Conflict." *Yahoo News*, August 15, 2022. https://news.yahoo.com/ war-ukraine-highlights-growing-strategic-123900157.html.

Bowen, Matt. "Why the United States Should Remain Engaged on Nuclear Power: Geopolitical and National Security Considerations." *Columbia SIPA Center on Global Energy Policy*, September 2020. https://www.energypolicy.columbia.edu/sites/default/files/file- uploads/Nuclear_Geopolitics_CGEP_Commentary_FINAL.pdf.

Bradstock, Felicity. "China Accounts for Nearly Half of the World's Renewable Energy Capacity." *Oil Price*, August 21, 2022. https:// oilprice.com/Energy/Energy-General/China-Accounts-For-Nearl y-Half-Of-The-Worlds-Renewable-Energy-Capacity.html.

Brigham, Katie. "How Three Companies Are Cleaning up the World's Plastic-Choked Rivers." *CNBC*, August 3, 2022. https://www.cnbc. com/2022/08/03/how-to-clean-the-worlds-most-polluted-rivers.html.

Brinkhof, Tim. "Did War Help Societies Become Bigger and More Complex?" *Big Think*, July 25, 2022. https://bigthink.com/the-past/ war-civilization-development/.

Button, Adam. "There Is a Profound Disconnect in Battery Metals." *Forexlive*, August 9, 2022. https://www.forexlive.com/news/there-i s-a-profound-disconnect-in-battery-metals-20220809/.

Byrn, Jimmy. "What if They Gave a War and Everybody Was Woke?" *Wall Street Journal*, July 29, 2022. https://www.wsj.com/articles/what-if-they-gave-a-war-and-ever ybody-was-woke-military-recruitment-crt-training-obesity -reading-labor-market-11659108526?mod=djemalertNEWS.

Cacciatore, Luca. "China, Russia to Engage in Joint Military Exercise." *Newsmax*, August 17, 2022. https://www.newsmax.com/newsfront/ china-russia-military-exercise/2022/08/17/id/1083550/.

Cairns, Christopher. "China's Investment Setbacks in Panama." *The Diplomat*, February 26, 2022. https://thediplomat.com/2022/02/ chinas-investment-setbacks-in-panama/.

Carlton, Jim, Matthew Dalton, and Sha Hua. "Droughts Hurt World's Largest Economies." *Wall Street Journal*, August 21, 2022. https://www.wsj.com/articles/droughts-hurt-worlds-largest-economies-11661087554?mod=mhp.

Carter, Dylan. "Russian Forces Threaten to Blow up Europe's Largest Nuclear Reactor." *Brussels Times*, August 8, 2022. https://www.brusselstimes.com/268817/russian-forces-threaten-to-blow-up-europes-largest-nuclear-reactor.

Cassella, Carly. "It's Literally Raining 'Forever Chemicals', and the Storm Could Last for Decades." *Science Alert*, August 5, 2022. https:// www.sciencealert.com/it-s-raining-forever-chemicals-and-some-researchers-argue-there-s-no-going-back.

CGTN, "Chinese, Canadian FMs Vow to Bring Bilateral Relations 'Back on Track.'" July 9, 2022. https://news.cgtn.com/news/2022-07-09/Chinese-Canadian-FMs-vow-to-bring-bilateral-relations-back -on-track--1bwt5TipN04/index.html.

CGTN, "China, Chile Vow to Push Bilateral Relations to Higher Level." August 17, 2022. https://news.cgtn.com/news/2022-08-17/China-Chile-vow-to-push-bilateral-relations-to-higher-level-1cznygRWlhe/index.html.

CGTN, "China, India Hold 16th Corps Commander Level Meeting on Border Issues." July 19, 2022. https://news.cgtn.com/news/2022-07-19/China-India-hold-16th-corps-commander-level-meeting-on-border-issues-1bMQ7aTx3Fu/index.html.

CGTN, "China Is World's 2nd Largest Commercial Satellite Owner." August 12, 2022. https://news.cgtn.com/news/2022-08-12/China-is-world-s-2nd-largest-commercial-satellite-owner-1cqEZjfndny/index.html.

CGTN, "China, Uzbekistan to Hold 6th Meeting of Intergovernmental Cooperation Committee." August 17, 2022. https://news.cgtn.com/news/2022-08-17/China-Uzbekistan-to-hold-6th-meeting-of-cooperation-committee-1czIhO79Q8o/index.html.

Chang, Gordon G. "Awaken to the China Threat: President Biden and America Must Understand the Dangers Posed by Our Asian Competitor." *Daily News*, November 14, 2021. https://www.nydailynews.com/opinion/ny-oped-awaken-to-the-china-threat-20211114-ppjokrcllza3vk7rw4edlk2bom-story.html.

Chan, Michelle. "SEC Adds Alibaba to List of Chinese Companies Facing Delisting." *Wall Street Journal*, July 29, 2022. https://www.wsj.com/articles/sec-adds-alibaba-to-list-of-chinese-companies-facing-delisting-11659130698.

Chaturvedi, Amit. "'World War III Has Begun after Sinking of Moskva': Russian State TV." *NDTV*, April 16, 2022. https://www.ndtv.com/world-news/world-war-iii-has-begun-after-sinking-of-moskva-russian-state-tv-2890945.

Chatzky, Andrew, and James McBride. "China's Massive Belt and Road Initiative." *Council on Foreign Relations*, January 1, 2020. https://www.cfr.org/backgrounder/chinas-massive-belt-and-road-initiative.

Chernov, Mstyslav. "Afghanistan Shrivels in Worst Drought in Decades." *The Diplomat*, December 10, 2021. https://thediplomat.com/2021/12/afghanistan-shrivels-in-worst-drought-in-decades/.

Chirileasa, Andrei. "Water Flow on the Danube Is One-Third of What It Should Be This Time of Year." *Romania-Insider*, July 25, 2022. https://www.romania-insider.com/danube-flow-romania-low-july-2022.

Clark, Colin. "Upstart Anduril Australia Hopes to Make 100s of Large Drone Subs, 'ITAR Free,' CEO Says." *Breaking Defense*, August 19, 2022. https://breakingdefense.com/2022/08/upstart-anduril-australi a-hopes-to-make-100s-of-large-drone-subs-itar-free-ceo-says/.

Clemons, Jay. "Putin Offers 'Most Advanced' Weapons to Socialist Triad in Latin America." *Newsmax*, August 16, 2022. https://www.newsmax.com/newsfront/russia-us-ukraine/2022/08/16/id/1083402/.

Clemons, Jay. "UN Report: China's Mistreatment of Uyghurs Akin to Modern Slavery." *Newsmax*, August 17, 2022. https://www.newsmax.com/newsfront/united-nations-china-uyghurs/2022/08/17/id/1083560/.

Clifford, Catherine. "Nuclear Power Is on the Brink of a $1 Trillion Resurgence, But One Accident Anywhere Could Stop That Momentum." *CNBC*, August 3, 2022. https://www.cnbc.com/2022/08/03/nuclear-energy-growing-popularity-could-be -undone-by-one-accident.html.

Clifford, Catherine. "Russian and Chinese Designs Dominate Nuclear Reactors, Warns IEA Chief." *CNBC*, July 1, 2021. https://www.cnbc.com/2022/07/01/russian-and-chinese-designs-in-87percen t-of-new-nuclear-reactors-iea-chief.html#:~:text=Russian%20 and%20Chinese%20designs%20dominate%20nuclear%20 reactors%2C%20warns%20IEA%20chief,-Published%20 Fri%2C%20Jul&text=Since%202017%2C%2087%25%20of%20 the,market%20leadership%2C%E2%80%9D%20Birol%20said.

Clifford, Catherine. "The Energy in Nuclear Waste Could Power the U.S. for 100 Years, but the Technology Was Never Commercialized." *CNBC*, June 2, 2022. https://www.cnbc.com/2022/06/02/nuclea r-waste-us-could-power-the-us-for-100-years.html.

Colby, Elbridge A., and Alexander B. Gray. "America's Industrial Base Isn't Ready for War with China." *Wall Street Journal*, August 18, 2022. https://www.wsj.com/articles/americas-industrial-bas e-isnt-ready-for-war-with-china-weapons-defense-funding-milit ary-war-conflict-taiwan-supplier-11660833718?mod=mhp.

Cole, Brendan. "Putin Suffers Black Sea Crisis as Russia Loses $750M Flagship, Jets, Island." *Newsweek*, August 16, 2022.

https://www.newsweek.com/black-sea-putin-crimea-snake-island-moskva-1734124.

Cole, Brendan. "Russian TV Airs Nuclear Missile Warning for U.S., Britain." *Newsweek*, August 9, 2022. https://www.newsweek.com/russia-ukraine-missiles-nuclear-warning-zaporizhzhya-britain-us-1732059.

Copp, Tara. "US Military 'Furiously' Rewriting Nuclear Deterrence to Address Russia and China, STRATCOM Chief Says." *Defense One*, August 11, 2022. https://www.defenseone.com/threats/2022/08/us-military-furiously-rewriting-nuclear-deterrence-address-russia-and-china-stratcom-chief-says/375725/.

Creitz, Charles. "Biden Officials Push Electric Cars on Recession-Weary Americans from Their 'Policy Fantasyland': Expert." *Fox News*, August 21, 2022. https://www.foxnews.com/media/biden-officials-push-electric-cars-recession-wary-americans-policy-fantasyland-expert.

Croker, Natalie, Renée Rigdon, Judson Jones, Carlotta Dotto, and Angela Dewan, "The World's Rivers Are Drying Up from Extreme Weather. See How 6 Look from Space." *CNN*, August 20, 2022. https://www.cnn.com/2022/08/20/world/rivers-lakes-drying-up-drought-climate-cmd-intl/index.html.

Cronin, Brittany. "How a Massive Refinery Shortage Is Contributing to High Gas Prices." *NPR*, June 26, 2022. https://www.npr.org/2022/06/26/1107265390/refinery-shortage-high-gas-prices-russia.

Daniel, Will. "China Just Ran into Something That Could Be Even More Devastating for Its Supply Chains than COVID-19 Lockdowns: A record Heat Wave." *Fortune*, August 20, 2022. https://fortune.com/2022/08/20/china-heatwave-supply-chain-covid-lockdowns/.

Danqwal, Ashish. "US Goes the 'Hypersonic-Way' to Develop Next-Gen Artillery; Tests 'Air-Breathing' Shells for Its Howitzers." *Eurasian Times*, August 10, 2022. https://eurasiantimes.com/us-goes-the-hypersonic-way-to-develop-next-gen-artillery/?amp.

Daunton, Nichola. "Illegal Fishing and Physical Violence: Life aboard China's 'Devil Vessels' Revealed in New Report." *Euronews.*

green, updated August 4, 2022. https://www.euronews.com/green/2022/04/08/illegal-fishing-and-physical-violence-life-aboard-china-s-devil-vessels-revealed-in-new-re.

Davidson, Helen. "China Warns US after Tracking Warship in South China Sea." *The Guardian*, January 1, 2022. https://www.theguardian.com/world/2022/jan/20/china-warns-of-serious-consequences-after-tracking-us-warship.

Dawson, Bethany. "Putin Accused the US of Acting like God and Predicted a New World Order in Bullish St Petersburg Speech." *Business Insider,* June 18, 2022. https://www.businessinsider.com/putin-us-god-over-ukraine-crisis-new-world-order-coming-2022-6.

Delbert, Caroline. "This Tiny Modular Nuclear Reactor Just Got the Green Light from U.S. Regulators." *Yahoo Finance*, August 3, 2022. https://finance.yahoo.com/news/tiny-modular-nuclear-reactor-just-184500363.html.

De Luce, Dan, and Ken Dilanian. "China's Growing Firepower Casts Doubt on Whether U.S. Could Defend Taiwan." *NBC News,* March 27, 2021. https://www.nbcnews.com/politics/national-security/china-s-growing-firepower-casts-doubt-whether-u-s-could-n1262148.

Demarest, Colin. "US Army Sets Timeline for Demo of New, Hard-to-Detect Mobile Command Post." *Army Times*, July 27, 2022. https://www.armytimes.com/c2-comms/2022/07/27/us-army-sets-timeline-for-demo-of-new-hard-to-detect-mobile-command-post/.

Devore, Chuck. "Thanks to Leftist Corruption, U.S. Military Recruiting Is in Total Freefall." *The Federalist*, June 29, 2022. https://thefederalist.com/2022/06/29/thanks-to-leftist-corruption-u-s-military-recruiting-is-in-total-freefall/.

DNA Web Team. "DNA Special: Has World War III Already Begun?" *DNA*, April 19, 2022. https://www.dnaindia.com/analysis/report-dna-special-has-world-war-iii-already-begun-2947040.

Domonoske, Camila. "How China Dominates the Electric Vehicle Supply Chain." *NPR*, February 21, 2022. https://www.npr.org/2022/02/21/1082172649/how-china-dominates-the-electri

c-vehicle-supply-chain#:~:text=DOMONOSKE%3A%20In%20
fact%2C%20when%20it,on%20China%20for%20these%20minerals.

Dow, "Dow, X-Energy to Drive Carbon Emissions Reductions through Deployment of Advanced Small Modular Nuclear Power." August 9, 2022. https://corporate.dow.com/en-us/news/press-releases/dow--x-energy-to-drive-carbon-emissions-reductions-through-deplo.

Dreyer, June Teufel. "Hong Kong Two Years after the Passage of the National Security Act." *Foreign Policy Research Institute*, June 6, 2022. https://www.fpri.org/article/2022/06/hong-kong-two-years-after-the-passage-of-the-national-security-act/.

Dube, Ryan. "The Place with the Most Lithium Is Blowing the Electric-Car Revolution." *Wall Street Journal*, August 10, 2022. https://www.wsj.com/articles/electric-cars-batteries-lithium-triangle-latin-america-11660141017?mod=mhp.

Dunleavy, Jerry. "Inside TikTok's Army of Lobbyists of Ex-Senators, Congressmen, and Staffers." *Washington Examiner*, July 31, 2022. https://www.washingtonexaminer.com/policy/technology/tiktok-lobbyists-gop-and-democrat-senators-congressmen-staffers.

Dupont, Alan. "The US-China Cold War Has Already Started." *The Diplomat*, July 8, 2020. https://thediplomat.com/2020/07/the-us-china-cold-war-has-already-started/.

Eaglen, Mackenzie. "Recruitment Is Now a Real Threat to a Frail Force Facing Formidable Foes." *Breaking Defense*, August 12, 2022. https://breakingdefense.com/2022/08/recruitment-is-now-a-real-threat-to-a-frail-force-facing-formidable-foes/.

Ebrahim, Hudhaifa. "Chinese President Due in Saudi Arabia to Tighten Economic Ties." *Jerusalem Post*, August 15, 2022. https://www.jpost.com/international/article-714744.

Economist, The. "America's Top Brass Responds to the Threat of China in the Pacific." March 11, 2021. https://www.economist.com/asia/2021/03/11/americas-top-brass-responds-to-the-threat-of-china-in-the-pacific?utm_medium=cpc.adword.pd&utm_source=google&utm_campaign=a.22brand_pmax&utm_content=conversion.

direct-response.anonymous&gclid=EAIaIQobChMIyIvCk7SH-QIVcgF9Ch10ogArEAMYASAAEgKAE_D_BwE&gclsrc=aw.ds.

Eckstein, Megan. "New US Marine Regiment Shows Off Capabilities at RIMPAC ahead of Fall Experimentation Blitz." *Defense News*, August 10, 2022. https://www.defensenews.com/naval/2022/08/10/new-us-marine-regiment-shows-off-capabilities-at-rimpac-ahead-of-fall-experimentation-blitz/.

Eckstein, Megan. "RIMPAC Lessons Will Inform Navy's Pursuit of a Program-of-Record Unmanned Ship in 2025." *Defense News,* August 1, 2022. https://www.defensenews.com/naval/2022/08/01/rimpac-lessons-will-inform-navys-pursuit-of-a-program-of-record-unmanned-ship-in-2025/.

Eckstein, Megan. "US Navy Injects First-of-Kind Unmanned Experiments into Multinational Exercise." *Yahoo News*, August 8, 2022. https://news.yahoo.com/us-navy-injects-first-kind-150000255.html.

Editorial Board, The. "Manchin's Mountain Valley Pipeline Dream." *Wall Street Journal*, August 2, 2022. https://www.wsj.com/articles/joe-manchins-mountain-valley-pipeline-dream-democrats-environmental-permitting-reforms-chuck-schumer-11659476809?mod=mhp.

Editorial Board, The. "Tilting at Climate Windmills. Schumer-Manchin Will Have Little Effect on the World's Temperature." *Wall Street Journal*, August 8, 2022. https://www.wsj.com/articles/tilting-at-climate-windmills-chuck-schumer-joe-manchin-tax-climate-bill-bjorn-lomborg-11659993292?mod=mhp.

Ellis, Michael. "China Is No. 1 Domestic National Security Threat and Biden Administration Won't Admit It." *Fox News,* July 29, 2022. https://www.foxnews.com/opinion/china-domestic-national-security-threat-biden.

Erwin, Sandra. "As DoD Shifts to Smaller Satellites, Rideshare Questions Emerge." *Space News*, August 18, 2022. https://spacenews.com/as-dod-shifts-to-smaller-satellites-new-questions-emerge-on-how-to-manage-rideshare-launches/.

Erwin, Sandra. "Commercial Geospatial Technologies That Detect GPS Disruptions to Be Tested in Military Exercises."

Space News, August 17, 2022. https://spacenews.com/
commercial-geospatial-technologies-that-detect-gps-disrupt
ions-to-be-tested-in-military-exercises/.

Erwin, Sandra. "DARPA Selects Companies for Inter-Satellite Laser Communications Project." *Space News*, August 10, 2022. https://spacenews.com/darpa-selects-companies-for-inter-satellite-laser-co mmunications-project/.

Erwin, Sandra. "SpaceX Gets $1.9 Million Air Force Contract for Starlink Services in Europe and Africa." *Space News*, August 15, 2022. https://spacenews.com/spacex-gets-1-9-million-air-force-cont ract-for-starlink-services-in-europe-and-africa/.

Erwin, Sandra. "U.S. Space Command Basing Decision Approaching Final Stretch." *Space News*, August 9, 2022. https://spacenews.co m/u-s-space-command-basing-decision-approaching-final-stretch/.

Evergreen, Shel. "'Elephant in the Room': Clean Energy's Need for Unsustainable Minerals." *Ars Technica*, May 2, 2022. https://arstechnica.com/science/2022/05/elephant-in-the-room-clea n-energys-need-for-unsustainable-minerals/.

Everington, Keoni. "China Warns US Not to Include Taiwan in Indo-Pacific Strategy." *Taiwan News*, February 22, 2022. https://www. taiwannews.com.tw/en/news/4451661.

Eversden, Andrew. "Army Must Start 'Leaning' on Kinetic Options for Counter-Drone as Autonomous UAS Proliferate." *Breaking Defense*, August 11, 2022. https://breakingdefense. com/2022/08/army-must-start-leaning-on-kinetic-options-for-cou nter-drone-as-autonomous-uas-proliferate/.

Eversden, Andrew. "'Bullet Made out of Light': Army to Field First Stryker-Mounted Combat Laser in Next 45 Days." *Breaking Defense*, August 10, 2022. https://breakingdefense.com/2022/08/bullet-mad e-out-of-light-army-to-send-first-stryker-mounted-combat-laser-to-soldiers-in-next-45-days/.

Evers-Hillstrom, Karl. "'Shocked and Disheartened': How Coal Country Is Reacting to Manchin's Climate Deal." *The Hill*, August 13, 2022. https://thehill.com/business-a-lobbying/3597520-shocked-a

nd-disheartened-how-coal-country-is-reacting-to-manchins-climate
-deal/.

ExxonMobil. "Renewable Diesel for Our Changing World." *Wall Street
Journal*, August 7, 2022. https://partners.wsj.com/exxonmobil/
business-of-carbon-capture-and-storage/renewable-diesel-for-ou
r-changing-world/?dclid=CJOmlsrktPkCFUtdwQod4g0AwA.

Faulconbridge, Guy, and Parisa Hafezi. "Putin Forges Ties with Iran's
Supreme Leader in Tehran Talks." *Reuters*, July 19, 2022. https://
www.reuters.com/world/putin-visits-iran-first-trip-outside-former
-ussr-since-ukraine-war-2022-07-18/.

Farberov, Snejana. "Putin's State TV Propagandist Olga Skabeyeva
Says 'World War III Has Already Begun.'" *New York Post*, June 1,
2022. https://nypost.com/2022/06/01/putin-propagandist-olga-sk
abeyeva-says-world-war-iii-has-already-begun/.

Faucon, Benoit, and Joe Parkinson. "Russian Mercenaries Project the
Kremlin's Power Far from Its Troubles in Ukraine." *Wall Street
Journal*, August 21, 2022. https://www.wsj.com/articles/russia-wagne
r-group-mercenaries-mali-west-africa-11661099199?mod=mhp.

FBI. "The China Threat." Accessed July 20, 2022. https://www.fbi.gov/
investigate/counterintelligence/the-china-threat.

Felbab-Brown, Vanda. "The China Connection in Mexico's Illegal
Economies." *Brookings*, February 4, 2022. https://www.brookings.
edu/opinions/the-china-connection-in-mexicos-illegal-economies/.

Feng, Rebecca. "The Bursting Chinese Housing Bubble Compounds
Beijing's Economic Woes." *Wall Street Journal*, August 11, 2022.
https://www.wsj.com/articles/bursting-chinese-housing-bubbl
e-compounds-beijings-economic-woes-11660235003.

Filseth, Trevor. "Game of Drones: Iran Hosts UAV Competition with
Russia and Belarus." *National Interest*, August 16, 2022. https://
nationalinterest.org/blog/middle-east-watch/game-drones-iran-host
s-uav-competition-russia-and-belarus-204246.

Finley, Allysia. "China Gets a Great Leap Forward from Congress."
Wall Street Journal, August 14, 2022. https://www.wsj.com/
articles/beijing-gets-a-great-leap-forward-from-congress-inflat

ion-reduction-act-green-energy-subsidies-innovation-price-contr
ols-capitalism-xi-jinping-11660502287?mod=mhp.

Fitzgerald, Sandy. "Tshibaka to Newsmax: Alaskans 'Very Concerned' over
NORAD Report." *Newsmax*, August 12, 2022. https://www.newsmax.
com/newsmax-tv/kellytshibaka-norad-russia/2022/08/12/id/1082883/.

Flatt, Courtney, and Laura Sullivan. "The U.S. Made a Breakthrough
Battery Discovery—Then Gave the Technology to China." *NPR*,
August 3, 2022. https://www.npr.org/2022/08/03/1114964240/
new-battery-technology-china-vanadium.

Fox News Staff, "Democrats' Inflation Reduction Act Is 'Economic
Malpractice': Economist." *Fox News*, August 6, 2022. https://
www.foxnews.com/politics/democrats-inflation-reductio
n-act-economic-malpractice-economist.

Frangoul, Anmar. "Goldman Sachs Doesn't See Nuclear as a
Transformational Technology for the Future." *CNBC*, August
5, 2022. https://www.cnbc.com/2022/08/05/goldman-doesnt-se
e-nuclear-as-a-transformational-tech-for-the-future.html.

Frayer, Lauren. "Why a Chinese Ship's Arrival in Sri Lanka Has Caused
Alarm in India and the West." *NPR*, August 19, 2022. https://www.
npr.org/2022/08/19/1118113095/sri-lanka-china-ship-hambantot
a-port.

Fromer, Jacob. "Next North Korea Nuclear Test Could Lead US to
Deploy 'Strategic Assets' to South Korea, Two Allies Say." *South
China Morning Post*, August 18, 2022. https://www.scmp.com/news/
china/military/article/3189277/next-north-korea-nuclear-test-could-
lead-us-deploy-strategic.

Fung, Katherine. "Russian Families Descend on the Kremlin to Demand
Truth about Soldiers." *Newsweek*, July 26, 2022. https://www.newsweek.
com/russian-families-descend-kremlin-demand-truth-about-so
ldiers-1728116.

Gabriel, Angeli. "How a Florida Nuclear Power Plant Became a
Crocodile Nursery." *Fox Weather*, August 1, 2022. https://www.
foxweather.com/earth-space/florida-crocodiles-nuclear-plant-turkey-
point?cmpid=hp1r_foxweather_obtest&dicbo=v1-7f5198ed1b5fe28

43114fa1af7c580c2-00e17b74303517cbe6bf08cea931e9f870-gmzw
czjrgiytcllfgvsgcljumzsgmljyg42dellggfqwcnjqgbstey3fmy.

Galston, William A. "America Wakes Up to the China Threat." *Wall Street Journal,* March 9, 2021. https://www.wsj.com/articles/americ a-wakes-up-to-the-china-threat-11615311587.

Gardner, Timothy. "U.S. Selects Test Plant for Advanced Nuclear Reactor Fuel." *Reuters*, July 27, 2022. https://www.reuters.com/ business/energy/us-selects-test-plant-advanced-nuclear-reac tor-fuel-2022-07-27/.

Gavlak, Dale. "UN, Experts Warn of Serious Water Problems for Iraq." *VOA*, June 20, 2022. https://www.voanews.com/a/un-experts-war n-of-serious-water-problems-for-iraq-/6625446.html.

Gehrke, Joel. "Japan Fears Putin Will Bring Nuclear Bombs Back to Battlefield." *Washington Examiner*, August 1, 2022. https:// www.washingtonexaminer.com/policy/defense-national-security/ japan-fears-putin-nuclear-bombs.

Gehrke, Joel. "Russian Embassy Praises Chinese Drone as 'Symbol of Modern Warfare.'" *Washington Examiner*, August 15, 2022. https:// www.washingtonexaminer.com/policy/defense-national-security/ russia-china-drone-ukraine-warfare.

Gehrke, Joel. "Russia Threatens to Sabotage European Nuclear Power Plants." *Washington Examiner*, August 12, 2022. https://www. washingtonexaminer.com/policy/defense-national-security/russi a-threatens-sabotage-european-nuclear.

Geiger, Julianne. "German Chancellor: Germany Could Keep Nuclear Power Plants Operating after All." *Oil Price*, August 3, 2022. https:// oilprice.com/Latest-Energy-News/World-News/German-Chancello r-Germany-Could-Keep-Nuclear-Power-Plants-Operating-After- All.html.

Gicheru Kinyua, Brian. "Drought Threatens Major Rivers in the U.S. and Europe." *Maritime Executive*, July 29, 2022. https:// maritime-executive.com/article/drought-threatens-major-river s-in-the-u-s-and-europe.

Gillispie, Mark. "Billions Pour into Bioplastics as Markets Begin Ramping Up." *AP News*, August 8, 2022. https://apnews.com/article/climate-and-environment-8dd0e4ad3345387ea72e83a506ef3a00.

Grady, John. "China's Navy Could Have 5 Aircraft Carriers, 10 Ballistic Missile Subs by 2030 Says CSBA Report." *USNI News*, August 18, 2022. https://news.usni.org/2022/08/18/chinas-navy-could-have-5-aircr aft-carriers-10-ballistic-missile-subs-by-2030-says-csba-report.

Grady, John. "Mattis: U.S. Suffering 'Strategic Atrophy.'" *USNI News*, May 14, 2015. https://news.usni.org/2015/05/14/mattis-u-s-suffering-strategic-atrophy.

Green Science Policy Institute, "It's Raining PFAS: Even in Antarctica and on the Tibetan Plateau, Rainwater Is Unsafe to Drink." August 2, 2022. https://phys.org/news/2022-08-pfas-antarctic a-tibetan-plateau-rainwater.html.

Hadley, Greg. "Air Force Official: We're 'Starting to Lose Our Lead' in Propulsion." *Air Force Magazine*, August 16, 2022. https://www.airforcemag.com/air-force-official-were-startin g-to-lose-our-lead-on-propulsion/.

Hamilton, Keegan. "Inside the Fight over California's Last Nuclear Power Plant." *Vice News*, August 4, 2022. https://www.vice.com/en/article/epzz87/california-nuclear-power-climate-change.

Hancock, Elaina. "For Advance Drought Warning, Look to the Plants." *Science X*, August 5, 2022. https://phys.org/news/2022-08-advance-drought.html.

Harel, Amos. "Russia-Ukraine War Catapults Israeli Arms Industry to Global Stage." *Haaretz*, August 5, 2022. https://www.haaretz.com/israel-news/security-aviation/2022-08-05/ty-article/.highlight/russia-ukraine-war-catapults-israeli-arms-industry-to-global-stage/00000182-69d0-d9e1-a1ae-f9f3637e0000.

Heckman, Elizabeth. "Idaho Sheriff Sends Dire Warning to 'Idiotic' Biden Officials: 'We Are on the Cusp of Complete Collapse.'" *Fox News*, July 27, 2022. https://www.foxnews.com/media/idaho-sherif f-sends-dire-warning-idiotic-biden-officials-cusp-complete-collapse.

Heinrich, Mark, ed. "Iran's Military Warns U.S. against Threats to Use Force." *Reuters*, July 15, 2022. https://www.reuters.com/world/middle-east/iran s-military-warns-us-against-threats-use-force-2022-07-15/.

Hiebert, Murray. "The Looming Environmental Catastrophe in the South China Sea." *The Diplomat*, January 14, 2022. https:// thediplomat.com/2022/01/the-looming-environmental-catastrophe- in-the-south-china-sea/.

Hoffman, Gabriella. "An Inconvenient Truth: ESG Is Fueling Inflation Woes." *Real Clear Energy*, July 29, 2022. https://www.realclearenergy. org/articles/2022/07/29/an_inconvenient_truth_esg_is_fueling_ inflation_woes_845052.html.

Honrada, Gabriel. "China, South Korea Racing for Stealth Fighter Supremacy." *Asia Times*, August 1, 2022. https://asiatimes.com/2022/08/ china-south-korea-racing-for-stealth-fighter-supremacy/.

Honrada, Gabriel. "China Unveils Game-Changing Electronic Warfare Drones." *Asia Times*, August 8, 2022. https://asiatimes.com/2022/08/ china-unveils-game-changing-electronic-warfare-drones/.

Honrada, Gabriel. "Guam's Missile Defenses to Get a Massive Upgrade." *Asia Times*, August 19, 2022. https://asiatimes.com/2022/08/guam s-missile-defenses-to-get-a-massive-upgrade/.

Honrada, Gabriel. "US Points New-Gen Missile Defense Radar at China, Russia." *Asia Times*, August 12, 2022. https://asiatimes.com/2022/08/ us-points-new-gen-missile-defense-radar-at-china-russia/.

Huang, Echo. "Asia's Rivers Send More Plastic into the Ocean than All Other Continents Combined." *Quartz*, June 14, 2017. https:// qz.com/1004589/80-of-plastic-in-the-ocean-can-be-traced-back-to -asias-rivers-led-by-china-indonesia-myanmar-a-study-by-nether land-based-the-ocean-cleanup-found/.

Huang, Zheping. "Chinese President Xi Jinping Has Vowed to Lead the 'New World Order.'" *Quartz*, February 22, 2017. https://qz.com/916382/chinese-president-xi-jinping-ha s-vowed-to-lead-the-new-world-order/.

Irfan, Umair. "How the Western Drought Is Pushing the Power Grid to the Brink." *VOX*, August 16, 2022. https://www.vox.com/23292669/

drought-2022-power-energy-grid-lake-mead-climate-heat-hoov
er-dam.

Jacobo, Julia. "Sea Level Rise Is Expected to Worsen Coastal Flooding—
Even on Sunny Days, According to New NOAA Report." *ABC
News*, August 3, 2022. https://abcnews.go.com/US/sea-level-ris
e-expected-worsen-coastal-flooding-sunny/story?id=87874281.

Jenkins, Holman W. "Why Pretend Green Pork Will Stop Climate Change?"
Wall Street Journal, July 29, 2022. https://www.wsj.com/articles/
why-pretend-green-pork-will-stop-climate-change-alternative-ener
gy-global-warming-lies-government-officials-11659129705?mod=mhp.

Jennings, Daniel G. "US Small Modular Reactor Production Can Begin."
Medium, August 3, 2022. https://marketmadhouse.medium.com/
us-small-modular-reactor-production-can-begin-b01a0547545c.

Jennings, Ralph. "China Cuts Tariffs, Cozies up to 16 of World's
Poorest Nations with US, Australia Trade Ties Strained." *SCMP*,
August 8, 2022. https://www.scmp.com/economy/global-economy/
article/3188149/china-cuts-tariffs-cosies-16-worlds-poorest-nations-
us?module=perpetual_scroll_0&pgtype=article&campaign=3188149.

Jerusalem Post Staff. "Russian Navy Should Be Equipped with Tactical
Nukes, Says Russian Scientist." *Jerusalem Post*, August 19, 2022.
https://www.jpost.com/omg/article-715100.

Judson, Jen. "Missile Defense Agency Priorities Include Hypersonics,
Guam, Hill Says." *Yahoo News*, August 12, 2022. https://news.yahoo.
com/missile-defense-agency-priorities-hypersonics-192404898.html.

Judson, Jen. "US Army Digs New Sandbox for Laser Weapons."
Defense News, August 18, 2022. https://www.defensenews.com/
digital-show-dailies/smd/2022/08/18/the-us-army-digs-a-new-
sandbox-for-its-laser-weapons/.

Kadam, Tanmay. "China Develops 'Anti-Stealth Radar' so Small That
It Could Be Set Up Anywhere, Including Rooftops—Scientists."
EurAsian Times, August 20, 2022. https://eurasiantimes.com/chin
a-develops-anti-stealth-radar-so-small-that-it-could/.

Kaplan, Seth D. "How China's Propaganda Influences the West." *Wall
Street Journal*, August 21, 2022. https://www.wsj.com/articles/ho

w-chinas-propaganda-influences-the-west-state-media-cable-censor
ship-wechat-social-media-hong-kong-election-russia-ukraine-new
spaper-11661108182?mod=mhp.

Katz, Justin. "Lockheed Delivers High-Energy Laser Four Years in the Making to US Navy." *Breaking Defense,* August 18, 2022. https:// breakingdefense.com/2022/08/lockheed-delivers-high-energy-laser -four-years-in-the-making-to-us-navy/.

Katz, Justin. "Russia's Naval Doctrine May Call for Challenging the West, but Does It Have the Shipyards?" *Breaking Defense*, August 19, 2022. https://breakingdefense.com/2022/08/russias-naval-doctrin e-may-call-for-challenging-the-west-but-does-it-have-the-shipyards/.

Kemp, Ted, and Lee Ying Shan. "U.S. Navy Is Seeing More 'Unsafe' Aerial Intercepts by China, Says Seventh Fleet Commander." *CNBC*, August 16, 2022. https://www.cnbc.com/2022/08/16/increase-i n-unsafe-aerial-chinese-intercepts-us-navy.html.

Kennedy, Charles. "Asia Gobbles up Cheap U.S. Crude at OPEC's Expense." *Oil Price*, August 12, 2022. https://oilprice.com/Energy/ Crude-Oil/Asia-Gobbles-Up-Cheap-US-Crude-At-OPECs- Expense.html.

Kennedy, Charles. "Russia Displaces Saudi Arabian Oil in India." *Oil Price*, August 5, 2022. https://oilprice.com/Energy/Crude-Oil/Russi a-Displaces-Saudi-Arabian-Oil-In-India.html.

Kenney, Caitlin M. "The Army Brief: Guam Missile Defense; CENTCOM Contest; New Social-Media Rules; and More." *Defense One*, August 19, 2022. https://www.defenseone.com/ threats/2022/08/the-army-brief-august-19-2022/376066/.

Kenney, Caitlin M. "US Navy Sail toward a Less-Crewed Future." *Defense One*, August 3, 2022. https://www.defenseone.com/ technology/2022/08/robot-ships-debut-rimpac-helping-us-navy- sail-toward-less-crewed-future/375305/.

Kerber, Ross. "Exclusive: Missouri Attorney General Investigates Morningstar over ESG Ratings." *Reuters*, August 3, 2022. https://www. reuters.com/business/sustainable-business/exclusive-missouri-attorne y-general-investigates-morningstar-over-esg-ratings-2022-08-03/.

Khaled, Fatma. "Putin Ally Lukashenko Faces Revolt from Officers against Ukraine War: Report." *Newsweek*, July 10, 2022. https://www.newsweek.com/putin-ally-lukashenko-faces-revolt-officers-against-ukraine-war-1723224.

Kimani, Alex. "How Commodity Traders Are Helping Fund Russia's War." *Oil Price*, August 2, 2022. https://oilprice.com/Energy/Energy-General/How-Commodity-Traders-Are-Helping-Fund-Russias-War.html.

Kimani, Alex. "Offshore Drilling Is Coming Back with a Bang." *Oil Price*, August 8, 2022. https://oilprice.com/Energy/Energy-General/Offshore-Drilling-Is-Coming-Back-With-A-Bang.html.

Kim, Anthony B. "Why Economic Freedom Is More Integral to Foreign Policy than Ever." *Washington Examiner*, May 5, 2022. https://www.washingtonexaminer.com/restoring-america/courage-strength-optimism/why-economic-freedom-is-more-integral-to-foreign-policy-than-ever.

Kine, Phelim. "Xi Jinping's Saudi Trip Seeks to Exploit Riyadh-Washington Tensions." *Politico*, August 16, 2022. https://www.politico.com/news/2022/08/16/xi-jinping-saudi-arabia-trip-middle-east-influence-00052023.

Knight, Ben. "Graphene Oxide Membranes Reveal Unusual Behavior of Water at the Nanoscale." *Science X*, August 5, 2022. https://phys.org/news/2022-08-graphene-oxide-membranes-reveal-unusual.html.

Knox, Brady. "Russia Announces Temporary Withdrawal from New START Treaty." *Washington Examiner*, August 8, 2022. https://www.washingtonexaminer.com/policy/foreign/russia-announces-temporary-withdrawal-new-start-treaty.

Kolker, Alexander S. "A New Storm Is Brewing in Struggle over Climate Change: Homeowner's Insurance." *The Hill*, August 2, 2022. https://thehill.com/opinion/energy-environment/3583414-a-new-storm-is-brewing-in-struggle-over-climate-change-homeowners-insurance/.

Landen, Xander. "Putin Knows He Made 'Mistake' with Ukraine, Will Never Admit It: Stavridis." *Newsweek*, August 14, 2022. https://www.newsweek.com/putin-knows-he-made-mistake-ukraine-wil

l-never-admit-it-stavridis-1733490?amp=1#amp_tf=From%20
%251%24s&aoh=16606682097702&csi=0&referrer=https%3A%2
F%2Fwww.google.com.

Lederer, Edith M. "UN Nuclear Chief: Ukraine Nuclear Plant Is 'Out of Control.'" *AP News*, August 3, 2022. https://apnews.com/article/russia-ukraine-science-accidents-d2e0077af104f2692b76f737c58e1984.

Lee Hotz, Robert. "Which Countries Create the Most Ocean Trash?" *Wall Street Journal*, February 12, 2015. https://www.wsj.com/articles/which-countries-create-the-most-ocean-trash-1423767676.

Lee, Howard. "Solving the Rock-Hard Problem of Nuclear Waste Disposal." *Ars Technica*, August 17, 2022. https://arstechnica.com/science/2022/08/solving-the-rock-hard-problem-of-nuclear-waste-disposal/.

Lee, Michael. "Russia Uses FBI Trump Raid to 'Foment Discord' and 'Amplify Tensions' in US, Expert Says." *Fox News*, August 14, 2022. https://www.foxnews.com/world/russia-uses-fbi-trump-raid-foment-discord-amplify-tensions-us.

Lee, Michael. "Taiwan Rejects China's 'One Country, Two Systems' Plan for the Island." *Fox News*, August 11, 2022. https://www.foxnews.com/world/taiwan-rejects-chinas-one-country-two-systems-plan-island.

Lee, Michael. "Western Tech Continues to Flow into Russia Despite Sanctions: Report." *Fox News*, August 8, 2022. https://www.foxnews.com/world/western-tech-continues-flow-russia-despite-sanctions-report.

Lendon, Brad. "'New Normal' across the Taiwan Strait as China Threat Looms Ever Closer." *CNN*, August 19, 2022. https://www.cnn.com/2022/08/19/china/china-taiwan-strait-new-normal-mic-intl-hnk-ml/index.html.

Leung, Hannah. "Five Asian Countries Dump More Plastic into Oceans than Anyone Else Combined: How You Can Help." *Forbes*, August 10, 2022, https://www.forbes.com/sites/hannahleung/2018/04/21/five-asian-countries-dump-more-plastic-than-anyone-else-combined-how-you-can-help/?sh=7c210d441234.

Loop, Emma. "Western Companies in China and Russia Eye Exits." *Washington Examiner*, July 21, 2022. https://www.washingtonexaminer.com/news/western-companies-in-china-and-russia-eye-exits.

Lovett, Ian. "Ukraine's Southern Forces Wage a Slow Campaign to Wear the Russians Down." *Wall Street Journal*, August 19, 2022. https://www.wsj.com/articles/ukraines-southern-forces-wage-a-slow-campaign-to-wear-the-russians-down-11660906801?mod=mhp.

Mack, Eric. "Russian Defense Minister: 'Soon Soviet Union Will Return.'" *Newsmax*, July 28, 2022. https://www.newsmax.com/newsfront/russia-defense-minister/2022/07/28/id/1080844/.

Mahadzir, Dzirhan. "U.S. Joins South Korea, Australia, Japan, Canada for Missile Defense Exercise Following RIMPAC." *USNI News*, August 16, 2022. https://news.usni.org/2022/08/16/u-s-joins-south-korea-australia-japan-canada-for-missile-defense-exercise-following-rimpac.

Maishman, Elsa. "Ukraine War Round-Up: Strike on Wagner HQ and Russia to Increase Ties with North Korea." *BBC News*, August 16, 2022. https://www.bbc.com/news/world-europe-62550437.

Majeed, Zaini. "'Day Will Come Soon': China Threatens US of Hawaii Incursion for Entering South China Sea." *Republic World*, September 13, 2021. https://www.republicworld.com/world-news/rest-of-the-world-news/day-will-come-soon-china-threatens-us-of-hawaii-incursion-for-entering-south-china-sea.html.

Martin, Nik. "Why China's Economy Is in Trouble and What It Means for You." *DW*, August 17, 2022. https://www.dw.com/en/why-chinas-economy-is-in-trouble-and-what-it-means-for-you/a-62823625.

Matthew, James Michael. *Reject Self-Serving Power*, Bloomington, IN: Archway Publishing, 2022. See esp. chap. 21, "Serendipity Pools for Climate Change."

Mayar, Assem. "Global Warming and Afghanistan: Drought, Hunger and Thirst Expected to Worsen." *Afghanistan Analysts Network*, November 6, 2021. https://www.afghanistan-analysts.org/en/reports/economy-development-environment/global-warming-and-afghanistan-drought-hunger-and-thirst-expected-to-worsen/.

Mazzucchi, Nicolas. "Nuclear Power Can Help the Democratic World Achieve Energy Independence." *Nature*, June 8, 2022. https://www. nature.com/articles/d41586-022-01733-9.

McFadden, Christopher. "China Allegedly Developed a New 'Flying Submarine' Drone That Could Penetrate Aircraft Carrier Defenses." *Interesting Engineering*, August 9, 2022. https://interestingengineering. com/innovation/china-allegedly-developed-a-new-flying-subma rine-drone-that-could-penetrate-aircraft-carrier-defenses.

McFadden, Christopher. "In a Show of Strength, the U.S. Has Once Again Tested Its Minuteman III ICBMs." *Interesting Engineering*, August 16, 2022. https://interestingengineering.com/innovation/ us-military-tests-minuteman-intercontinental-missile.

McFall, Caitlan. "World Economic Forum Calls to Reduce Private Vehicles by Eliminating 'Ownership.'" *Fox Business*, July 28, 2022. https://www.foxbusiness.com/economy/world-economic-forum-call s-reduce-private-vehicles-by-eliminating-ownership.

McNamara, Ryan. "The Environmental Collateral Damage of the South China Sea Conflict." *New Security Beat*, November 13, 2020. https:// www.newsecuritybeat.org/2020/10/environmental-collateral-damage- south-china-sea-conflict/.

Michta, Andrew A. "China, Russia, and the West's Crisis of Disbelief." *Wall Street Journal*, August 7, 2022. https://www.wsj.com/articles/chin a-russia-and-the-wests-crisis-america-democracy-fight-military-threat -disarmament-cold-war-putin-xi-response-11659892566?mod=mhp.

Miller, Andrea. "Why the Global Soil Shortage Threatens Food, Medicine and the Climate." *CNBC*, June 5, 2022. https://www. cnbc.com/2022/06/05/why-the-global-soil-shortage-threatens-f ood-medicine-and-the-climate.html.

Miller, Andy. "EPA Action Boosts Grassroots Momentum to Reduce Toxic 'Forever Chemicals.'" *Atlanta Journal-Constitution*, August 8, 2022. https://www.ajc.com/life/health/epa-action-boosts-grassroots- momentum-to-reduce-toxic-forever-chemicals/JJHMK7ZN65AELG 55CHPQFRBKH4/.

Mion, Landon. "Hundreds of Mexican National Guard Troops Sent to Tijuana over Cartel-Fueled Violence." *Fox News*, August 14, 2022. https://www.foxnews.com/world/hundreds-mexican-national-guard-troops-sent-tijuana-over-cartel-fueled-violence.

Mizokami, Kyle. "Ramjet-Powered Artillery Will Make U.S. Ground Forces More Fearsome Than Ever." *Yahoo News*, August 12, 2022. https://news.yahoo.com/ramjet-powered-artillery-u-ground-161000010.html.

Mongilio, Heather. "U.S. Will Continue Taiwan Strait Transits, FONOPs in Western Pacific Despite Growing Tension with China." *USNI News*, August 8, 2022. https://news.usni.org/2022/08/08/u-s-will-continue-taiwan-strait-transits-fonops-in-western-pacific-despite-growing-tension-with-china.

Moore, Mark. "China Threatens Nuclear War, Expanding Arsenal in Case of 'Intense Showdown' with US." *New York Post*, June 2, 2021. https://nypost.com/2021/06/02/chinese-media-says-beijing-expanding-its-nuclear-arsenal/.

Moss, Trefor. "The Key to Electric Cars Is Batteries. One Chinese Firm Dominates the Industry." *Wall Street Journal*, November 3, 2019. https://www.wsj.com/articles/how-china-positioned-itself-to-dominate-the-future-of-electric-cars-11572804489.

Nava, Victor I. "Petraeus: Afghanistan Likely Will Be 'Incubator for Islamist Extremism' for Years." *Washington Examiner*, August 9, 2022. https://www.washingtonexaminer.com/news/petraeus-afghanistan-incubator-islamist-extremism.

Nava, Victor I. "Russia Launches Iranian Satellite into Space." *Washington Examiner*, August 9, 2022. https://www.washingtonexaminer.com/news/watch-russia-launches-iranian-satellite-into-space.

NEI. "Advanced Nuclear." Accessed August 13, 2022. https://www.nei.org/fundamentals/advanced-nuclear.

Nelson, Felicity. "A Huge Step forward in Quantum Computing Was Just Announced: The First-Ever Quantum Circuit." *Science Alert*, June 22, 2022. https://www.sciencealert.com/

a-huge-step-forward-in-quantum-computing-was-just-anno
unced-the-first-ever-quantum-circuit.

Neuman, Scott. "China's Military Drills around Taiwan Show How It Is Closing the Gap with the U.S." *NPR*, August 5, 2022. https://www.npr.org/2022/08/05/1115731152/china-taiwan-military-drills-pelosi-visit.

Newsfront. "'China Threat' Emerges in Elections from UK to Australia." *Newsmax*, August 14, 2022. https://www.newsmax.com/newsfront/elections-the-china-card/2022/08/14/id/1083028/.

Newsmax. "China Plans Cloud Seeding to Protect Grain Crop amid Drought." August 21, 2022. https://www.newsmax.com/world/globaltalk/china-drought/2022/08/21/id/1083944/.

Nexus Media. "Top Coal Firm in World Cashing in on Global Energy Crisis." *Clean Technica*, August 11, 2022. https://cleantechnica.com/2022/08/10/top-coal-firm-in-world-cashing-in-on-global-energy-crisis/amp/#amp_tf=From%20%251%24s&aoh=16602525225421&csi=0&referrer=https%3A%2F%2Fwww.google.com.

Nissenbaum, Dion. "Iran Has Begun Training Russia to Use Its Advanced Drones, U.S. Says." *Wall Street Journal*, August 10, 2022. https://www.wsj.com/articles/iran-has-begun-training-russia-to-use-its-advanced-drones-u-s-says-11660135921.

Nolan, Beatrice. "Demand Is so High for the Legendary Bayraktar Drones Used to Defend against Russia's Ukraine Invasion that Their Turkish Maker Has a 3-Year Waitlist." *Business Insider*, August 15, 2022. https://www.businessinsider.com/baykar-drone-ukraine-manufacturing-factory-demand-bayraktar-tb2-drones-2022-8.

Nolan, Beatrice. "Europe's Energy Crisis Has Gotten so Bad That French Power Stations Are Being Allowed to Break Environmental Rules as a Fresh Heatwave Looks Set to Cause More Chaos." *Business Insider*, August 9, 2022. https://www.businessinsider.com/energy-french-power-stations-environmental-rules-heatwave-europe-2022-8.

Novak, Dan. "Satellites Show Landfills Releasing Large Amount of Methane." *VOA* News, August 14, 2022. https://learningenglish.

voanews.com/a/satellites-show-landfills-releasing-large-amount-of-methane/6697742.html.

Novelly, Thomas. "Space Force Takes Over All Military Satellite Communications." *Yahoo News*, August 15, 2022. https://news.yahoo.com/space-force-takes-over-military-185337796.html.

O'Connell, Gerard. "Pope Francis: 'World War III Has Been Declared.'" *America*, June 14, 2022. https://www.americamagazine.org/politics-society/2022/06/14/pope-francis-war-ukraine-nato-243153.

Office of Nuclear Energy. "5 Facts about Spent Nuclear Fuel." March 30, 2020. https://www.energy.gov/ne/articles/5-fast-facts-about-spent-nuclear-fuel.

O' Grady, Mary Anastasia. "Iran and a Suspicious Flight to Argentina." *Wall Street Journal*, July 17, 2022. https://www.wsj.com/articles/iran-and-a-suspicious-flight-to-argentina-airplane-crew-passports-investigation-jet-cyber-intelligence-venezuelan-agents-11658078058?mod=mhp.

O'Neill, Patrick Howell. "Hackers Linked to China Have Been Targeting Human Rights Groups for Years." *MIT Technology Review*, August 16, 2022. https://www.technologyreview.com/?p=1057894&preview=true&truid=&utm_source=the_download&utm_medium=email&utm_campaign=the_download.unpaid.engagement&utm_term=Active%20Qualified&utm_content=08-16-2022&mc_cid=4c2a4b06e2&mc_eid=7f625e5060.

Osborn, Kris. "DF-26: The Navy Has Plans to Destroy China's Best 'Carrier Killer' Missile." *National Interest*, August 15, 2022. https://nationalinterest.org/blog/buzz/df-26-navy-has-plans-destroy-china%E2%80%99s-best-%E2%80%98carrier-killer%E2%80%99-missile-204202.

Ownes, Mackubin. "The Marines of the Future." *Washington Examiner*, April 7, 2022. https://www.washingtonexaminer.com/politics/the-marines-of-the-future.

Oxford Business Group. "Emerging Markets Rush to Join BRICS Alliance as High Energy Prices Persist." *Oil Price*, August 21, 2022. https://oilprice.com/Geopolitics/International/Emerging-Markets-Rush-To-Join-BRICS-Alliance-As-High-Energy-Prices-Persist.html.

Panasovskyi, Maksim. "Lockheed Martin Is the First in the World to Deliver the HELIOS Laser Weapon—It Works on the Principle of the 'Death Star.'" *Gagadget.com*, August 18, 2022. https://gagadget.com/en/weapons/158998-lockheed-martin-is-the-first-in-the-world-to-deliver-the-helios-laser-weapon-it-works-on-the-principle-of-the-dea/#.

Panasovskyi, Maksim. "Northrop Grumman Received $3.29 Billion to Develop a Missile Defense System that Could Protect the Entire U.S. Territory from Ballistic Missiles." *Gagadget.com*, April 8, 2022. https://gagadget.com/en/war/154089-northrop-grumman-received-329-billion-to-develop-a-missile-defense-system-that-could-protect-the-entire-us-territory-/.

Panasovskyi, Maksim. "Saudi Arabia Bought the Best American THAAD Air Defense System for $15 billion and Will Prepare Four Sites for Them by 2026." *Gagadget.com*, August 20, 2022. https://gagadget.com/en/weapons/159229-saudi-arabia-bought-the-best-american-thaad-air-defense-system-for-15-billion-and-will-prepare-four-sites-for-the/.

Panasovskyi, Maksim. "Switzerland Will Abandon the American M109 KAWEST Howitzer in Favor of the Swedish Archer or German RCH 155 AGM." *Gagadget.com*, August 16, 2022. https://gagadget.com/en/war/157773-switzerland-will-abandon-the-american-m109-kawest-howitzer-in-favor-of-the-swedish-archer-or-german-rch-155-agm/.

Pandey, Ashutosh. "Chinese Graphite Dominance Threatens Electric Car Ambitions." *Deutsche Welle*, March 14, 2022. https://www.dw.com/en/chinese-graphite-dominance-threatens-electric-car-ambitions/a-60888876.

Papadopooulos, Loukia. "Watch Lockheed Martin Test Its Layered Laser Defense System." *Interesting Engineering*, August 13, 2022. https://interestingengineering.com/innovation/lockheed-martin-layered-laser-defense-system.

Paraskova, Tsvetana. "Bill Gates-Backed Firm Raises $750M to Develop Small Nuclear Reactors." *Oil Price*, August 15, 2022. https://oilprice.com/Latest-Energy-News/World-News/Bill-Gates-Backed-Firm-Raises-750M-To-Develop-Small-Nuclear-Reactors.html.

Paraskova, Tsvetana. "Global Refining Capacity to Expand with New Projects in Middle East, Asia." *Oil Price*, August 2, 2022. https://oilprice.com/Latest-Energy-News/World-News/Global-Refining-Capacity-To-Expand-With-New-Projects-In-Middle-East-Asia.html.

Paraskova, Tsvetana. "High-Impact Oil and Gas Drilling Is Back." *Oil Price*, August 21, 2022. https://oilprice.com/Energy/Crude-Oil/High-Impact-Oil-And-Gas-Drilling-Is-Back.html.

Paraskova, Tsvetana. "Money Won't Solve America's Power Grid Problems." *Oil Price*, August 15, 2022. https://oilprice.com/Energy/Energy-General/Money-Wont-Solve-Americas-Power-Grid-Problems.html.

Paulsson, Lars. "France to Curb Nuclear Output as Europe's Energy Crisis Worsens." *Bloomberg*, August 3, 2022. https://www.bloomberg.com/news/articles/2022-08-03/edf-to-curb-nuclear-output-as-french-energy-crisis-worsens.

Pegden, Tom. "Rolls-Royce Working on $300m US Department of Defense Contract to Build Transportable Micro Nuclear Reactor." *Business Live*, August 4, 2022. https://www.business-live.co.uk/manufacturing/rolls-royce-working-300m-department-24662057.

Pflughoeft, Aspen. "Centuries-Old Warnings Emerge from Riverbed as Europe Faces Historic Drought." *Miami Herald*, August 12, 2022. https://www.miamiherald.com/news/nation-world/world/article264446131.html.

Philip, Lizzie. "Why the US Needs Russian Uranium." *The Verge*, August 9, 2022. https://www.theverge.com/2022/8/9/23283165/russia-ukraine-war-us-uranium.

Phippen, Thomas. "Tax and Climate Bill Could Massively Expand IRS Union, Which Almost Exclusively Donates to Democrats." *Fox News*, August 11, 2022. https://www.foxnews.com/politics/tax-climate-bill-massively-expand-irs-union-almost-exclusively-donates-democrats.

Pike, Lili. "China Is Owning the Global Battery Race." *GRID*, January 18, 2022. https://www.grid.news/story/global/2022/01/18/china-is-owning-the-global-battery-race-that-could-be-a-problem-for-the-us/.

Post Editorial Board. "Biden's Created Our Bad New Normal, and He's Loving It." *New York Post*, August 13, 2022. https://nypost.com/2022/08/13/bidens-created-our-bad-new-normal-and-hes-loving-it/.

Post Editorial Board. "Germany's Painful Lesson for US Climate Warriors on the Dangers of Going Green." *New York Post*, August 20, 2022. https://nypost.com/2022/08/20/germanys-painful-lesson-for-us-climate-warriors-on-the-dangers-of-going-green/.

Prescott, R. Jordan. "Goodbye Conventional War. It's Been Fun." *Modern War Institute at West Point*, March 21, 2019. https://mwi.usma.edu/goodbye-conventional-war-fun/.

Psaropoulos, John. "Ukrainian Attacks in Crimea Weaken Russia's Military Capacity." *Alijazeera*, August 18, 2022. https://www.aljazeera.com/news/2022/8/18/ukrainian-attacks-in-crimea-weaken-russias-military-capacity.

Qazizai, Fazelminallah. "In Afghanistan, a Drought Highlights the Climate Crisis." *New Lines*, June 15, 2022. https://newlinesmag.com/newsletter/in-afghanistan-a-drought-highlights-the-climate-crisis/.

Queen, Chris. "Gaslighting: How the Mainstream Media Tries to Drive You to the Left." *PJ Media*, August 6, 2022. https://pjmedia.com/columns/chris-queen/2022/08/06/gaslighting-how-the-mainstream-media-tries-to-drive-you-to-the-left-n1618882.

Rabouin, Dion. "U.S. Companies on Pace to Bring Home Record Number of Overseas Jobs." *Wall Street Journal*, August 20, 2022. https://www.wsj.com/articles/u-s-companies-on-pace-to-bring-home-record-number-of-overseas-jobs-11660968061?mod=mhp.

Reuters, "Factbox: Energy Crisis Revives Nuclear Power Plants Globally." August 4, 2022. https://www.reuters.com/business/energy/energy-crisis-revives-nuclear-power-plans-globally-2022-08-04/.

Reuters. "Plunging Water Levels of China's Yangtze Reveal Ancient Statues." *Yahoo News*, August 20, 2022. https://news.yahoo.com/plunging-water-levels-chinas-yangtze-182353400.html.

Reuters. "UK Summons Chinese Ambassador over 'Aggressive' Escalation on Taiwan." *Fox News*, August 10, 2022. https://

www.foxnews.com/world/uk-summons-chinese-ambassado
r-aggressive-escalation-taiwan.

Richard, Lawrence. "Daughter of Top Putin Ally Alexander Dugin, Who Pushed for Ukraine Invasion, Killed by Car Bomb outside Moscow." *Fox News*, August 21, 2022. https://www.foxnews.com/ world/daughter-top-putin-ally-alexander-dugin-pushed-ukraine -invasion-killed-car-bomb-outside-moscow.

Robertson, Harry. "China's Imports of US Oil Have Hit an 18-Month High as It Pivots away from Russian Crude." *Markets Insider*, August 17, 2022. https://markets.businessinsider.com/news/ commodities/china-imports-us-oil-rise-spurns-russian-crude-ene rgy-india-2022-8.

Rosen, Phil. "An Unknown Chinese Merchant Spends $376 Million on 13 Cargo Ships for Risky Russian Oil Transfers on the High Seas, Report Says." *Markets Insider*, August 11, 2022. https://markets. businessinsider.com/news/commodities/russian-oil-ship-to-shi p-transfer-anonymous-chinese-buyer-sanctions-2022-8.

Rosen, Phil. "Russian Crude Is Quietly Flowing to European Buyers like Italy and Spain as EU Sanctions Loom." *Markets Insider*, August 8, 2022. https://markets.businessinsider.com/news/ commodities/russian-oil-exports-italy-turkey-european-buyer s-sanctions-war-ukraine-2022-8?amp=#amp_tf=From%20% 251%24s&aoh=16600808152046&csi=0&referrer=https% 3A%2F%2Fwww.google.com.

Russell, Bethany G. "Economic Warfare." *Military Review* 100, no. 5 (September-October 2020): 33–43 https://www.armyupress. army.mil/Journals/Military-Review/English-Edition-Archives/ September-October-2020/Russell-Economic-Warfare/.

Russell, Walter. "A Costly Passivity toward China." *Wall Street Journal*, August 8, 2022. https://www.wsj.com/articles/a-costl y-passivity-toward-china-nancy-pelosi-taiwan-visit-military-bu ildup-diplomacy-pacific-japan-south-korea-investment-trade- security-11659991742?mod=mhp.

Saballa, Joe. "Spain Receives First THeMIS Unmanned Ground Vehicle." *The Defense Post*, August 11. 2022. https://www.thedefensepost. com/2022/08/11/spain-themis-unmanned-vehicle/amp/#amp_ tf=From%20%251%24s&aoh=16609246070711&csi=0&referrer= https%3A%2F%2Fwww.google.com.

Sabry, Mohamed. "Egypt to Build Desalination Plant in Iraq." *AL-Monitor*, June 28, 2022. https://www.al-monitor.com/originals/2022/06/egypt- build-desalination-plant-iraq.

Sahakian, Teny. "Climate Change Proposals Putting American Food Supply at Risk, Says Dairy Farmer." *Yahoo News*, August 4, 2022. https://news.yahoo.com/climate-change-proposals-puttin g-american-060053559.html.

Samuels, Ben, and Avi Scharf. "Dozens of IRGC-Linked Flights Landed in Moscow; U.S. Says Drone Deal Advancing." *Haaretz*, August 12, 2022. https://www.haaretz.com/israel-news/security- aviation/2022-08-12/ty-article/amid-drone-deal-irgc-linke d-flights-to-russia-surge/00000182-8bcc-da98-abf6-bfdd2d710000.

Sandia National Laboratories. "Back to the Drawing Board: Reinventing Offshore Wind Turbines." *TechXplore*, August 16, 2022. https:// techxplore.com/news/2022-08-board-reinventing-offshore-turbines. html.

Schauenberg, Tim. "Water Scarcity: EU Countries Forced to Restrict Drinking Water Access." *Deutsche Welle*, July 7, 2022. https://www. dw.com/en/water-scarcity-eu-countries-forced-to-restrict-drink ing-water-access/a-62363819.

Schultz, Teri. "Finns Say Yes to Nuclear Waste." *Deutsche Welle*, November 8, 2022. https://www.dw.com/en/finns-say-yes-to-nuclear-waste/a-62779844.

Sempa, Francis P. "Air Force Drag Queen Show Betrays the Military's Mission." *American Spectator*, August 4, 2022. https://spectator.org/ air-force-drag-queen-show-betrays-military-mission/.

Sganga, Nicole. "Chinese Hackers Took Trillions in Intellectual Property from about 30 Multinational Companies." *CBS News*, May 4, 2022. https://www.cbsnews.com/news/chinese-hackers-took-trillions-in-i ntellectual-property-from-about-30-multinational-companies/.

Shahab, Nabiha. "Indonesia Is Facing a Plastic Waste Emergency." *China Dialogue Ocean*, June 9, 2021. https://chinadialogueocean.net/en/pollution/17615-indonesias-plastic-waste-emergency/.

Shoaib, Alia. "Taiwan's 'Porcupine Strategy' to Fight a Potential Chinese Invasion Is Learning Lessons from Ukraine, Report Says." *Business Insider*, August 21, 2022. https://www.businessinsider.com/taiwan-learns-ukraine-porcupine-strategy-defend-against-china-2022-8.

Silverstein, Joe. "LA Times Urges Biden to Use Executive Powers to Declare a 'National Climate Emergency.'" *Fox News*, August 7, 2022. https://www.foxnews.com/media/la-times-urges-biden-use-executive-powers-declare-national-climate-emergency.

Slav, Irina. "How Russian Oil Is Making Its Way from Europe to Asia." *Oil Price*, August 1, 2022. https://oilprice.com/Energy/Crude-Oil/How-Russian-Oil-Is-Making-Its-Way-From-Europe-To-Asia.html.

Smith, Jessica. "GOP Congressman: Americans, Lawmakers Are 'Waking Up' to China Threat." *Yahoo Finance*, October 25, 2019. https://www.yahoo.com/video/gop-congressman-americans-lawmakers-are-waking-up-to-china-threat-135004552.html.

Smith, Jillian. "National Security Concerns Arise as China Buys Up U.S. Farmland." *Komo News*, August 13, 2022. https://komonews.com/amp/news/nation-world/national-security-concerns-arise-as-china-buys-up-us-farmland-investors-chinese-espionage-nations-food-security-at-risk-united-states-farms-usda-fufeng-group-usa.

South, Todd. "Marines Eying the Overlooked Individual Ready Reserve to Keep Talent." *Marine Times*, April 17, 2022. https://www.marinecorpstimes.com/news/your-marine-corps/2022/04/17/marines-eying-the-overlooked-individual-ready-reserve-to-keep-talent/.

Stanton, Andrew. "Putin Regime at 'Beginning of the End': Russia Expert." *Newsweek*, July 30, 2022. https://www.newsweek.com/putin-regime-beginning-end-russia-expert-1729402?_gl=1.

Stanway, David, and Muyu Xu. "China's Ocean Waste Surges 27% in 2018: Ministry." *Reuters*, October 29, 2019. https://www.reuters.com/article/us-china-pollution-oceans/chinas-ocean-waste-surges-27-in-2018-ministry-idUSKBN1X80FL.

Stimson, Brie. "US to Hold Wide-Ranging Trade Talks with Taiwan amid Tensions with China." *Fox News*, August 18, 2022. https://www.foxnews.com/world/us-hold-wide-ranging-trade-talks-taiwan-tensions-china.

Stop These Things, "Not Green: Offshore Wind 'Industry' Destroying Fishing Grounds, Birds & Marine Life." February 4, 2022. https://stopthesethings.com/2022/02/04/not-green-offshore-wind-industry-destroying-fishing-grounds-birds-marine-life/.

Strozewski, Zoe. "Putin Ally Promotes Nuclear Strike on NATO to Counter Military Superiority." *Newsweek*, August 16, 2022. https://www.newsweek.com/russian-tv-host-vladimir-solovyov-promotes-nuclear-strike-nato-counter-military-superiority-1734135.

Strozewski, Zoe. "Putin Scrambling for Support from 'Outcasts' Shows His Weakness: Expert." *Newsweek*, August 10, 2022. https://www.newsweek.com/putin-scrambling-support-outcasts-shows-his-weakness-expert-1732622.

Surran, Carl. "No New Refineries Likely Ever Built Again in the U.S., Chevron CEO Warns." *Seeking Alpha,* June 3, 2022. https://seekingalpha.com/news/3845705-no-new-refineries-likely-ever-built-again-in-the-us-chevron-ceo-warns.

Take, Sayumi. "China's Solar Panel Supply Chain Domination Cause for Worry: IEA." *NIKKEI Asia*, July 7, 2022. https://asia.nikkei.com/Business/Energy/China-s-solar-panel-supply-chain-domination-cause-for-worry-IEA#:~:text=China%20now%20holds%20a%20market,of%20global%20demand%2C%20it%20said.

Tandon, Kashish. "China Threatens to 'Hunt Down' US Military Jets if They Again Land in Taiwan." *EurAsian Times*, July 20, 2021. https://eurasiantimes.com/china-threatens-to-hunt-down-us-military-jets-if-they-again-land-in-taiwan/.

Tan, Huileng. "Germany Says It May Leave Its Final 3 Nuclear Energy Plants Running for Longer than Planned, Reversing Nearly a Decade of Work." *Business Insider*, July 28, 2022. https://www.businessinsider.com/germany-delay-nuclear-energy-plant-exit-russia-natural-gas-cut-2022-7.

Tan, Su-Lin. "'Dirty Ol' Coal' Is Making a Comeback and Consumption Is Expected to Return to 2013's Record Levels." *CNBC*, August 1, 2022. https://www.cnbc.com/2022/08/02/coal-consumption-is-expected-to-return-to-2013s-record-levels-iea.html.

Tan, Su-Lin. "G-7's Infrastructure Plan Offers an Alternative to China's Belt and Road Initiative in a 'Deliberate Way.'" *CNBC*, June 28, 20222. https://www.cnbc.com/2022/06/28/new-g-7-infrastructure-plan-offers-alternative-to-china-belt-road-.html.

Tatlow, Didi Kirsten. "China Targets Israeli Technology in Quest for Global Dominance as U.S. Frets." *Newsweek*, August 10, 2022. https://www.newsweek.com/2022/08/19/china-targets-israeli-technology-quest-global-dominance-us-frets-1727108.html.

Taylor, Chloe. "Bill Ackman Says Russia's Attack on Ukraine Means World War III Has Likely Already Started." *CNBC,* March 7, 2022. https://www.cnbc.com/2022/03/07/russia-ukraine-bill-ackman-says-world-war-iii-likely-already-started.html.

Taylor, Guy. "Iranian Dissidents Rally This Weekend in Albania as Washington-Tehran Tensions Surge." *Washington Times*, July 20, 2022. https://www.washingtontimes.com/news/2022/jul/20/iranian-dissidents-reject-wests-appeasement-policy/.

Their, Jane. "Gen Zers Turn to TikTok with Their Fantasies of Taking over Corporate America: 'Bring on the 4-Day Workweeks and 6-Hour Days.'" *Yahoo Finance*, August 1, 2022. https://finance.yahoo.com/news/gen-zers-turn-tiktok-fantasies-182653160.html.

Tipp Insights Editorial Board, "China Riding the 'Pink Tide' in South America." *Tipp Insights*, August 12, 2022. https://tippinsights.com/china-riding-the-pink-tide-in-south-america/.

TOI Staff. "Iran's 'Ambitious' Nuclear Program 'Moving Ahead Very, Very Fast,' Warns IAEA Head." *Times of Israel*, August 3, 2022. https://www.timesofisrael.com/iran-nuclear-program-moving-ahead-very-fast-warns-iaea-head/.

TOI Staff. "New Iran Satellite Presents Significant Challenge to Israel, US and Allies—Experts." *Times of Israel*, August 10, 2022. https://www.timesofisrael.com/new-iran-satellite-presents-significant-challenge-to-israel-us-and-allies-experts/.

Tong-Hyung, Kim. "China, South Korea Clash over THAAD Anti-Missile System." *Defense News*, August 10, 2022. https://www.defensenews.com/global/asia-pacific/2022/08/10/china-south-korea-clash-over-thaad-anti-missile-system/.

Towey, Hannah. "JPMorgan CEO Jamie Dimon: 'Why Can't We Get It through Our Thick Skulls?' America Boosting Oil and Gas Production Is 'Not Against' Climate Change." *Yahoo News*, August 14, 2022. https://news.yahoo.com/jpmorgan-ceo-jamie-dimon-why-145955451.html.

Tress, Luke. "Iran-Linked Hacking Group Is Targeting Israeli Shipping, US Cybersecurity Firm Says." *Times of Israel*, August 17, 2022. https://www.timesofisrael.com/iran-linked-hacking-group-targeting-israeli-shipping-us-cybersecurity-firm-says/.

Trinko, Myroslav. "ATACMS Replacement: Lockheed Martin Is Developing a New Missile for HIMARS and M270 with a Range of up to 650 km, It Will Be Able to Destroy Ships." *Gagadget.com*, August 6, 2022. https://gagadget.com/en/war/154802-atacms-replacement-lockheed-martin-is-developing-a-new-missile-for-himars-and-m270-with-a-range-of-up-to-650-km-it-wi/00.

Trofimov, Yaro. "Ukraine's Drone Spotters on Front Lines Wage New Kind of War." *Wall Street Journal*, August 7, 2022. https://www.wsj.com/articles/ukraines-drone-spotters-on-front-lines-wage-new-kind-of-war-11659870805.

Tsymbaliuk, Roman. "Russian Authorities Are Putting the Country's Defense Enterprises on a 24-Hour Work Schedule." *Ukrinform*, August 17, 2022. https://www.ukrinform.net/rubric-economy/3552107-russian-defense-industry-switching-to-247-operations.html.

Udasin, Sharon. "Scientists Link 'Forever Chemical' Exposure to Development of Liver Cancer." *The Hill*, August 8, 2022. https://thehill.com/policy/equilibrium-sustainability/3593017-scientists-link-forever-chemical-exposure-to-development-of-liver-cancer/.

Ukrinform. "Another Russian Spy Busted in Ukraine." August 19, 2022. https://www.ukrinform.net/amp/rubric-ato/3553771-another-russian-spy-busted-in-ukraine.html.

U.S. Department of State. "Forced Labor in China's Xinjiang Region." July 1, 2021. https://www.state.gov/forced-labor-in-chinas-xinjiang-region/.

Vernon, Will. "Ukraine War: Russia Appeals for New Recruits for War Effort." *BBC News*, August 22, 2022. https://www.bbc.com/news/world-europe-62553629.

Wang, Brian. "California and Germany Could Save Nuclear Reactors." *Next Big Future*, August 7, 2022. https://www.nextbigfuture.com/2022/08/california-and-germany-could-save-nuclear-reactors.html#amp_tf=From%20%251%24s&aoh=16600808152046&csi=0&referrer=https%3A%2F%2Fwww.google.com.

Wang, Brian. "France Will Spend 10 Billion Euros to Relaunch Nuclear Energy." *Next Big Future*, August 7, 2022. https://www.nextbigfuture.com/2022/08/france-will-spend-10-billion-euros-to-relaunch-nuclear-energy.html.

Watchers. "Rhine River Drops to Record Lows, Restricting Shipping and Exacerbating the European Energy Crisis." August 5, 2022. https://watchers.news/2022/08/05/rhine-river-drops-to-record-lows-restricting-shipping-and-exacerbating-the-european-energy-crisis/.

Week Staff, The. "Are We Heading for World War Three?" *The Week*, October 28, 2022. https://www.theweek.co.uk/92967/are-we-heading-towards-world-war-3.

Weinthal, Benjamin. "Palestinian Islamic Jihad's Rocket Barrages on Israel Trace back to 'Iran's Regional Tentacles,' Experts Say." *Fox News*, August 7, 2022. https://www.foxnews.com/world/palestinian-islamic-jihads-rocket-barrages-israel-trace-irans-regional-tentacles-experts-say.

Willis, Haisten. "Bold Bill or Terrible Tax Hike? Biden and GOP Fight to Define New Spending Law." *Washington Examiner*, August 18, 2022. https://www.washingtonexaminer.com/news/white-house/define-inflation-reduction-act.

Wilson, Simon. "How China Is Cornering the Market for Electric-Car Batteries." *Money Week*, January 8, 2022. https://moneyweek.com/investments/commodities/industrial-metals/604306/china-cobalt-electric-car-batteries.

Wingate, Sophie. "Blasts behind Russian Lines Had Major Psychological Effect on Putin—Officials." *Independent*, August 19, 2022. https://www.independent.co.uk/news/uk/vladimir-putin-crimea-ukraine-kremlin-jeremy-fleming-b2148556.html.

Winter, Jana. "Exclusive: U.S. Government Warns That Iran May Try to Kill American Officials as Revenge for Killing Top General." *Yahoo News*, July 13, 2022. https://news.yahoo.com/exclusive-u-s-government-warns-iran-may-try-to-kill-american-officials-in-revenge-for-killing-top-general-162641423.html.

WIRED. "Nuclear Power Plants Are Struggling to Stay Cool." *Ars Technica*, July 22, 2022. https://arstechnica.com/science/2022/07/nuclear-power-plants-are-struggling-to-stay-cool/?amp=1.

Wolf, Frank. "China Arrests Cardinal Zen and Religious Freedom Now Faces a Grim Future in Hong Kong." *Fox News*, August 21, 2022. https://www.foxnews.com/opinion/china-arrests-cardinal-zen-religious-freedom-faces-grim-future-hong-kong.

World Nuclear Association. "What Is Nuclear Waste, and What Do We Do with It?" Accessed August 17, 2022. https://world-nuclear.org/nuclear-essentials/what-is-nuclear-waste-and-what-do-we-do-with-it.aspx.

Wright, George. "Zaporizhzhia: Real Risk of Nuclear Disaster in Ukraine—Watchdog." *BBC News,* August 6, 2022. https://www.bbc.com/news/world-europe-62449982.

Xie, Echo. "China Is Building a Nuclear Power Plant in Argentina as It Looks to Latin America." *South China Morning Post*, February, 13, 2022. https://www.scmp.com/news/china/diplomacy/article/3166763/china-building-nuclear-power-plant-argentina-it-looks-latin.

Xie, John. "How China Dominates Global Battery Supply Chain." *VOA*, September 1, 2020. https://www.voanews.com/a/silicon-valley-technology_how-china-dominates-global-battery-supply-chain/6195257.html.

Xue, Yujie. "Chinese Green Ambitions' Dirty Side: Beijing Faces Recycling Challenge as Millions of Wind Turbines and Solar Panels near Retirement." *South China Morning Post*, August 7, 2022. https://www.scmp.com/business/article/3187849/chinese-green-ambition

s-dirty-side-beijing-faces-recycling-challenge?module=perpetual_
scroll_0&pgtype=article&campaign=3187849.

Yang, Zeyi. "Inside the Software That Will Become the Next Battle Front in US-China Chip War" *MIT Technology Review*, August 18, 2022. https://www.technologyreview.com/2022/08/18/1058116/ed a-software-us-china-chip-war/.

Yeryoma, Maria. "2 Years after Dictator Lukashenko Stole the Election, Belarus Is a Grim Place." *Kyiv Independent*, August 9, 2022. https:// kyivindependent.com/regional/two-years-after-dictator-lukash enko-stole-the-election-belarus-is-a-grim-place.

Yoon, Dasl. "U.S., South Korea Revive Live Military Drills after Four-Year Hiatus." *Wall Street Journal*, August 21, 2022. https://www. wsj.com/articles/u-s-south-korea-revive-live-military-drills-after-f our-year-hiatus-11661074202.

Zane, J. Peder. "The Physics of Freedom." *Real Clear Politics*, July 11, 2022. https://www.realclearpolitics.com/articles/2022/07/11/the_ physics_of_freedom_147865.html.

ZeroHedge. "Venezuela Halts Oil Shipments to Europe, Demands New Concessions." *Oil Price*, August 19, 2022. https://oilprice. com/Energy/Crude-Oil/Venezuela-Halts-Oil-Shipments-T o-Europe-Demands-New-Concessions.html.

Zhai, Keith. "China's Xi Considers Visiting Central Asia, Potential Meeting with Putin Next Month." *Wall Street Journal*, August 19, 2022. https:// www.wsj.com/articles/chinas-xi-considers-visiting-central-asia-pot ential-meeting-with-putin-next-month-11660916483?mod=mhp.

Zhai, Keith. "Southeast Asia Seeks to Tiptoe through U.S.-China Taiwan Minefield." *Wall Street Journal*, August 7, 2022. https:// www.wsj.com/articles/southeast-asia-seeks-to-tiptoe-through-u-s -china-taiwan-minefield-11659872556?mod=mhp.

Zisser, Eyal. "Iran Is Already Nuclearized, so Why Do We Need a Deal?" *Israel Hayom*, August 21, 2022. https://www.israelhayom.com/ opinions/iran-is-already-nuclearized-so-why-do-we-need-a-deal/.